C000100356

The Photographs of William Rayson Smith

Volume II

Dedicated to the memory of Ethnie Simnett and Rhoda & Basil Crowe

The Photographs of William Rayson Smith

Volume II:
Lowestoft

David Butcher

POPPYLAND
PUBLISHING

Copyright © David Butcher.

This edition 2020 published by Poppyland Publishing, Lowestoft, NR32 3BB.

www.poppyland.co.uk

ISBN 978 1 909796 78 2

All rights reserved. No part of this publication may be reproduced, stored in a retrieval system or transmitted by any means, mechanical, photocopying, recording or otherwise, without the written permission of the publishers.

Designed and typeset in 10.5 on 13.5 pt Times New Roman.

All images are from the William Rayson Smith collection © Jennifer and David Boxall except p.10 (bottom), which is in the collection of Matt Rix and the map on p.13 which is out of copyright.

Royalties from this book have been kindly donated by the author to Lowestoft lifeboat.

CONTENTS

PREFACE

The opportunity to produce a different kind of historical work does not often occur, and so to have this chance of presenting the photographs of William Rayson Smith which are focused on Lowestoft is a welcome challenge. Thanks are due, therefore, to Gareth Davies of Poppyland Publishing and to Jennifer and David Boxall for enabling me to take it up and being supportive, in a number of ways, regarding my attempts to do justice to the work of this most competent amateur photographer. Jennifer and David Boxall's tribute to the man (and his talent) formed the subject matter of Volume I—a record of life in the mid-Waveney Valley area of South Norfolk during the late 19th century, with an earlier period of time spent in Canada also represented. The photographs shown in this particular book were the result of WRS (as he will be referred to, from now on) visiting the town where his father lived in retirement, after a working life spent in the corn-milling trade at Dickleburgh.

WRS himself was born in 1841, and little is known of his domestic or working life, though he was obviously comfortably off, financially—probably as a result of the family business and perhaps also from marrying the daughter of a mill-owner from Harleston. Not long after the wedding, in 1868, he and his wife Maria (née Hudson) emigrated to Canada in 1870, settling in the town of Belleville at the eastern end of Lake Ontario. Both of them are recorded in the 1871 and 1881 Canadian census returns (WRS with the occupation of "clerk" in the latter), and it seems to have been during his time abroad that he took up photography. He and his wife had returned to England by 1887, bringing with them a girl aged twelve or thirteen named Winifred Colman, whose parents had Norfolk origins and who had younger siblings. She came to be regarded as the adopted daughter of WRS and his wife (childless themselves) and is described as such in the 1911 British census. The little family unit (for such it was) settled in Harleston, where Maria's brother Henry ran the family's milling business. After living at the *Mill House* until 1903, they then moved on to the *Magpie Inn* for a time and afterwards to a rented residence named *Elmhurst*. Maria died in 1924 and WRS in 1932. Winifred Colman lived on until 1962, unmarried—the Smiths' adopted daughter and beneficiary.

The surviving collection of photographs taken by WRS, which featured in Volume I, demonstrate a talent not only in the technical art of taking pictures, but in a sense of composition also. The subjects are perhaps what might be expected of a semi-leisured (perhaps even a wholly-leisured) man of means of the late 19th century, consisting of local views and events, family gatherings and occasions, visits to places beyond the immediate home-environment, and everyday working practices. As such, they combine to give a real sense of time and place in varying contexts, as well as some feeling perhaps for the man who captured these moments in time—not knowing the interest they would still hold for an audience nearly a century and a half removed from the era in which he lived. The same holds true of his Lowestoft images, which transport us back to a time when Queen Victoria was celebrating fifty years and more on the throne, when the British Empire was at its acme, and when the first of two world-shattering conflicts had yet to tear Europe apart.

In presenting this Lowestoft collection, an attempt has been made to accompany the images with substantial commentary, showing not only what can be seen in them but, also, what is there to be seen. The excellence of WRS's work lies not only in the immediate visual quality of his photographs, but in what they are able to tell us about the times in which he lived, in terms of the events taking place, the different activities recorded and the topographical significance of the locations seen. Each picture has a story to tell, beyond the particular and immediate view, and the writer has done his best to convey its detail. Context is everything in handling historic material of any kind—and there is a richness and depth in every single shot which must not be allowed to pass unnoticed. Photographs of this nature, taken at a particular time and in a particular place, have a value far beyond the merely visual and scenic. They are able to tell us a great deal about people's everyday lives and the world in which they found themselves. Photography does not only record time, place and event. It takes us beyond these into a wider experience, whereby we ourselves (looking in from the outside) can feel ourselves to be part of the great tide of history itself. A common saying declares that "every picture tells a story". Those that WRS has handed down tell many different ones, each time, within a single frame.

The Picture Collection

These two albums contain the whole body of the surviving photographic work of WRS, numbering 328 prints in all, of half-plate size. Forty-four of them relate to Lowestoft and its local area and two more to Great Yarmouth. These are the ones which form the subject matter of this book. The numbers appended to them in the text represent the order in which they are mounted (within their category) in the albums: nos. 1-26 in the first (begun during the late 1880s) and nos. 39-58 in the second (started c. 1890). In addition, WRS's captions are given below the photographs in italics. Both sets of images are preceded by, and interspersed with, other material—much of it forming the subject-matter of *The Photographs of William Rayson Smith: Vol. I, Norfolk and Beyond*. The albums themselves were described in Volume I (p. 10)—one of landscape proportions, the other pictorial. Each is bound in boards and leather and contains forty pages made of thick, light-brown card. The earlier one (landscape form) has been rebound at some point. A specific time-frame for the Lowestoft material, taken on the limited amount of dating evidence available, is 1887-92—but it was possibly longer than that. WRS obviously took the photographs during visits to see his father, who had retired to the town and who died there in December 1897.

It is interesting to note that, in some, ways, a number of the images which WRS has left us mirror the work of Harry Jenkins, a young professional photographer from Tunbridge Wells, who arrived in Lowestoft in 1896 and took over the Premises of H. Bevan (photographer) in Pier Terrace—being succeeded in successive generations by his son, Ford, and grandson, Peter. The work he did in recording the Lowestoft of his time, from the late 19th century into the 1920s and 30s, is an impressive and well-known one—as is that of his younger brother, Frederick, who operated in Southwold.

WRS and Tricycle

Here is the man himself, seated on a classic piece of Victorian light engineering—a tricycle (as also shown in Volume I, p. 65). The machine is beautifully constructed and of elegant lines and proportions, with a warning-bell close to the operator's left hand. A directly applied brake is visible above the front wheel (solid tyres all round) and the small chain-wheel shows that the gearing is sufficiently low, to avoid putting too great a strain on the legs when pedalling along. It is fair to assume that WRS may have worked up quite a sweat, when out on the roads of the time, given the heavy suit he is wearing. His close-fitting cap, with its small peak, is absolutely typical of its period and seen worn by so many sporting gentlemen in late 19th and early 20th century photographs.

A Family Occasion

This photograph shows a Smith family gathering in the back-garden of 16 Marine Parade, Lowestoft—the retirement home of WRS's father, William Snr., who is the focal point of the shot and may well have been celebrating his eightieth birthday (baptised 5 April 1812). While it was probably WRS's camera and tripod that were being used, he obviously wasn't the one to operate the shutter, as he is part of the group assembled. Back row: Anna Smith, Frederick Womack, WRS, Samuel Smith, Spencer Rix and Edward Eaton. Between the rows: Emma Womack (née Smith). Front row: Eliza Smith, Mary Rix (née Smith), William Smith Snr., Maria Smith (wife of WRS) and Joanna Eaton (née Smith). Sons-in-law Frederick Womack and Spencer Rix

were both farmers, originating from Fersfield and Thrandeston respectively, but based elsewhere in Norfolk when the picture was taken. Looking somewhat like the future Edward VII in this shot, Edward Eaton was in fact a chemist, with a business in Woodbridge, but his origins were also local to the Dickleburgh area—at Thelveton.

William Snr. probably moved into the house in June 1881, having married his third wife, Sarah Drake (widow), at Mutford during that month. She was owner of the property, having acquired it in March 1868 for the sum of £675 (c. £42,000 in today's values) from Anna Dalrymple of Norwich, widow of Arthur Dalrymple, the first occupant. A pre-nuptial agreement had been drawn up on 20 April 1881, allowing William to live in the house for term of his life, should Sarah pre-decease him—after which it was to pass to his daughter (and fifth child) Eliza. After Sarah died, in March 1888, Eliza (who had not married) became her father's housekeeper and inherited the property when he passed away, in December 1897—she being fifty-two years of age by then. An interesting factor in all of this is that the Census Return of 1881 (taken on 3 April) reveals that Sarah Drake had originated from Dickleburgh and that Eliza Smith was staying with her at the time. And so, William Smith had a long-established connection of some kind with her (though seven years her senior) through both of them having been born and raised in the same village community.

The 1911 Census shows Eliza still in occupation, with an older, unmarried sister, Anna (aged seventy-three), living with her. A visitor from Ashbrittle in Somerset (near Wellington), Elizabeth Harris—a widow of eighty-one years of age—was staying there at the time and a live-in servant, Gertrude Tussle, aged thirty-five (who came from Blundeston), was also part of the household. The three ladies are all described as being of "Private Means". Eliza Smith sold the house in May 1919 (for the sum of £600) to Rosa Norton, widowed member of a local, Lowestoft family of tobacconists, and she is referred to in the conveyance as being "of Redenhall"—thereby showing that she had returned to the area of South Norfolk from which she had originated, possibly to be near her older brother, WRS, who lived nearby in Harleston.

WRS In His Later Years

This fine studio head and shoulders portrait shows WRS in later life. His beard and moustache can't totally conceal the hint of a smile, and there is also perhaps a suggestion of a twinkle in his eye as he faces the camera. He not only knew how to take a good picture, but also how to face the camera when he himself was the subject.

Before leaving this Preface, it would be remiss of the writer if the assistance of other people was not acknowledged. Bob Malster has, as always, been helpful with details relating to Lowestoft's maritime activity—particularly in matters connected with the harbour and its mercantile operations, as well as in the fine details relating to the various types of craft seen in some of the photographs. Sue Barnard kindly contributed biographical material relating to Sarah Drake and William Kenney Patrick and to the latter's working life on the farms of Suffolk (**Town and Surrounds** section). John Stannard, of Lowestoft Civic Society and the town's Heritage Workshop Centre, provided very interesting material relating to the history of No. 16 Marine Parade and the origins of the terrace of which it forms part. And Ivan Bunn came up with details of the architectural work of John Louth Clemence—his interest in the man happily coinciding with that of the writer. All of these contributions have enriched the commentary and added to its level of interest. Any errors detected there will almost certainly be the fault of the author.

David Butcher, October 2020

INTRODUCTION

The decision made by William Smith Snr., miller of Dickleburgh, to retire from working life to a seaside residence in Lowestoft (during 1881), when he was sixty-nine years of age, was undoubtedly the causal factor in the creation of this book. Without that change of location, and the family connection it carried with it, WRS might never have had a direct motivation to visit the town and take the photographs he did. It is known that he and his wife had returned from Canada and were living in Harleston by 1887 (significantly, perhaps, the earliest year attached to any of his Lowestoft pictures) and trips to the Suffolk coast were, by then, conveniently possible by train. The Waveney Valley line (Tivetshall to Beccles) could be accessed at Harleston, followed by a change at Beccles to pick up a north-bound Ipswich train to Lowestoft—his father's home, at 16 Marine Parade, being about a quarter of a mile from the station.

The 1880s were an important and significant time in the history of Lowestoft. The town was reaching social and economic heights (created by activities of the preceding forty to fifty years) not previously experienced. In 1831, the town was still more or less contained within its old medieval limits—with all that this entailed in the way of overcrowding for many of the residents, caused by subdivision of the original house-plots and tenementation of older, larger dwellings. A later, overspill, residential area known as the "Beach Village" (*The Grit*, to its inhabitants) was developing on the southern part of the Denes, but most of the population was contained within what would today be described as "the High Street area". The population in 1831 was 4,238; by 1891, it had reached 19,150. Twenty years further on, it stood at 37,886!

The roots of this rapid expansion in the size of the town are to be found, initially, in the creation of a new piece of road during the early 1800s. This bypassed the circuitous, southwards route of the High Street, Old Nelson Street and what has long been called Battery Green Road and simply went in a straight line down to the shingle bank (between the sea and Lake Lothing) which carried the highway onwards into Kirkley, Pakefield and beyond. This is what is known today as London Road North and, once it had been finished, building plots began to form to either side of it. Even more important was the construction of the harbour (1827-30), under the supervising powers of the great Victorian-era civil engineer, William Cubitt (born at Dilham, in Norfolk, and also the son of a miller)—not carried out specifically with the idea of improving Lowestoft's long-established maritime activities, but to provide the vital part of an alternative navigational route to Norwich—the merchants of that city taking exception to what they regarded as the excessive tolls charged by the Great Yarmouth port authorities on both inward- and outward-bound cargoes.

This attempt to bypass Yarmouth (involving, also, the building of Mutford Lock, the canalisation of Oulton Dyke and the digging of the New Cut at Haddiscoe to link the River Waveney to the Yare) never really "took off" and by the early 1840s the harbour company found itself bankrupt. Norwich and Yarmouth had reached agreement regarding the matter of tolls; there was insufficient alternative maritime trade to make operations viable; and local fishing activity (although significant in size) was still very largely conducted off the North Beach area. Silting-up of the harbour mouth had been caused as early as 1839 by the teredo marine-worm attacking the timber of the sea-lock gates, thereby rendering these incapable of aiding the "flushing" effect of tidal flow to keep the bridge-channel clear of sediment. In 1843, a consortium of six local men took a chance on purchasing the whole of the harbour works from the Public Works Loan Commissioners, into whose hands the facility had fallen, and began to undertake some remedial repairs. A year later, they sold their interest out to Samuel Morton Peto, one of England's foremost builder-contractors of the 19th century.

Exactly how Peto came to see the economic and commercial potential of Lowestoft is not clear, but it was probably tied up with his railway interests and involvement in constructing parts of the growing national network. The town had a centuries-long connection with fishing (particularly for herring locally and, at one time, for Icelandic cod) and also with maritime trade to and from north European ports as far away as Riga—to say nothing of connections with Leghorn (Livorno), in Italy, and other Mediterranean stations. It had also developed a seasonal summer-resort function during the 1760s, with bathing machines in use on the North Beach and (later on) a bath-house where the local spring-water could work its medicinal magic! All of this was aimed at the upper echelons of local society, but at least one nationally significant grandee, Charles Sloane, third Baron Cadogan, had an imposing cliff-top residence built for his amenity and pleasure, in 1789—a residence today which is just plain No. 3 High Street. It was probably this leisure function which motivated Peto to purchase also the old manorial South Common (for the sum of £200)—an area of coastal heathland used primarily for the rough grazing of livestock, which lay to the south of the Inner Harbour and projected into the neighbouring parish of Kirkley. It was the seaward section of this which became a model resort of the mid-19th century, both in terms of its layout and its architecture.

It is commonly said, correctly, that Peto was the creator of modern Lowestoft, with his far-sighted investment in all three aspects of its maritime strengths (fishing, overseas trade and leisure opportunity) and the town's rapid population growth—as cited in the second paragraph of this introduction—was the result of his innovations. In a fifteen-year period, between 1844 and 1859, he improved the existing harbour facilities, built a new harbour on the seaward side of the existing road bridge (with fish markets and a cattle-landing area on the north pier and an amenity promenade along the south one), established a rail link with Norwich (1847) and, from thence, to other parts of the country, followed by another to Ipswich (1859) which created a direct route to London, and raised a sea-front esplanade to the south of the new harbour which rivalled any other of the time in the whole of the country. In addition to all of this (working in tandem with his associates, Lucas Brothers), he also purchased Somerleyton Hall, a local Jacobean-period country seat, and rebuilt it in fashionable Italianate style. Not satisfied with this alone, he also constructed a completely new, thatched-roof, model village of mock-Tudor character, set around a classic village-green on a space created from a major diversion of the road to Lowestoft. Both projects were carried out, using the designs of his London architect, John Thomas—also, an accomplished and acclaimed sculptor.

In 1862, he ran into severe financial difficulties, having overstretched himself with his many constructional projects all over the country, and he sold the Somerleyton estate as a means of raising capital and left the area. It is no part of this Introduction to give a detailed account of the career of Samuel Morton Peto, as a national figure, but to record his formative influence in raising Lowestoft from a moderately successful fishing-station and seaside watering-place into a coastal community of growing importance and significance. And it was not only in the spheres of increasing economic strength and population that the town made its mark, but in the matter of local government as well. Twenty years or more after Peto had left the locality, the town had become large and important enough to be awarded borough status. Its Charter of Incorporation was granted on 29 August 1885 and this enabled it to become a self-governing unit, with duly elected councillors (representing wards) and a mayor as civic head—moving it on from a residual governing system of manorial procedure, parochial administration and the work of Improvement Commissioners, thereby endowing it with a strong sense of civic identity and the confidence to believe that it had been given the recognition it deserved.

It was this new Lowestoft that WRS stepped into, with his camera and tripod, when he came to visit his father each time and it is, perhaps, to be regretted that he didn't capture more of it in the photographs he took. Or, if he did, then the work has not survived. As these pages unfold, it will not escape the attention of readers who live in the town, or who know it well, that the images are mainly those of locations within easy distance of where his father lived at 16 Marine Parade, being mainly focused on the Harbour and Fish Markets and on the Southern Esplanade—though even *Wellington Terrace* (al. *Esplanade*) is noticeably absent from the last-named. The main shopping-area of London Road North is not represented (except for one fragmentary part of it, incidental to a single photograph's subject), and there is no record of the High Street, and very little of the Denes situated below—other than two shots of one particular event taking place there. And perhaps most significant of all, given its character and photogenic quality, there is nothing which records the so-called "Beach Village"—*The Grit*, to everyone who lived there and to many other people in the town as well. That was certainly an opportunity missed for someone of WRS's talent. If, indeed, he did miss it. Likely or not, we just don't know and should, in any case, be thankful for what he has left us. We should all be much the poorer without it.

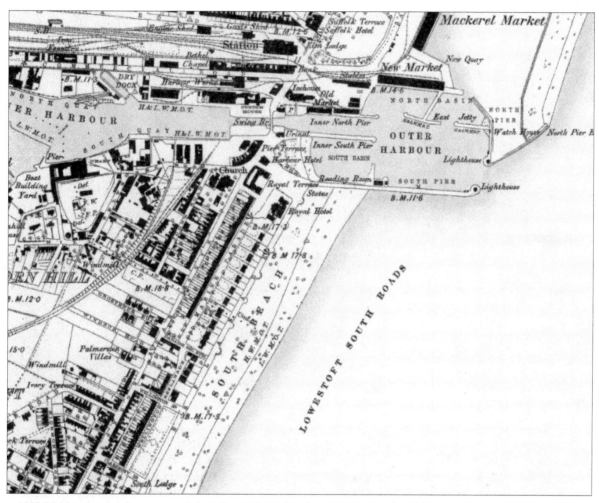

1885 OS Map showing the area around the harbour, The Esplanade and Marine Parade with its new villas.

COASTAL SCENES

2. A Steamship Offshore

From Beach Lowestoft

The vessel seen here was almost certainly anchored up off Lowestoft's North Beach, rather than its southern counterpart. The *Kirkley Roads*, as they had been known during the late medieval period, and then the *Lowestoft Roads* following that, were a favoured place for enabling vessels to lay in—either to land cargo onto the Denes or to take goods on board (before the harbour was built), or to break a sea-voyage and take on fresh water and supplies, or seek shelter on a friendly shoreline in stormy weather. In a coastal-defence survey of May 1545, against possible French invasion, Thomas Howard, third of his family as Duke of Norfolk, gave a detailed assessment of the whole stretch of water between the Stanford Channel (opposite Lowestoft) and the St. Nicholas Gat (opposite Great Yarmouth). He said that there was sufficient space for 500 ships to bring up, at low water, and safely remain there in all weathers.

The ship in this picture, like all the other images to follow, was taken within a time-frame of 1887-92 if the dated material is to be believed and it is a particularly unusual one within a Lowestoft context, being a sealing or whaling vessel of some kind. It is a typical dual-propulsion craft of the mid-late 19th century, with two masts and with the funnel amidships revealing the presence of a steam-engine also. Four or five good-sized whale-boats are visible on board, hung from davits. Whalers usually had three masts, so it looks as if the central one had been removed for some specific reason. The exaggerated overhang of the lute stern was designed to help the vessel ride high, following seas—but what it was doing here, off Lowestoft, can only be guessed at!

23. Salvaging of a Wreck, South Beach

Heaving wreck ashore Lowestoft

This image shows the final stages of retrieving a vessel driven ashore, close to the South Pier. A great deal of dismantling has already taken place, with only the lower part of the hull left, and a towing-line of some sort appears to be getting prepared to pull the remnants ashore. The main subject of the picture is clear enough, but the background is very faded (possibly due to processing of the shot, as much as its execution), but it is just possible to make out the somewhat ghostly outlines of the pier-heads on the right of the picture, beyond the hulk. As well as the men seen present, to carry out the final stages of retrieval, a number of boys are also in evidence—especially the ones to left of centre, sitting on the Pier's timber baulk to watch the action—but, at least not getting in the way! It looks very much as if the rope to be used in dragging the wreck ashore has still to be taken out and secured, and the rowing-boat in the foreground was probably there to carry it. Over the years (especially in the days of sail), a number of craft were driven ashore to the north and south of the harbour by strong onshore winds, one of the most notable and inconvenient of which was the smack *Sparkling Nellie* (LT 750), which foundered close to the north pierhead in the harbour's mouth itself, on 20 November 1902, and had to be blown up to clear the way for incoming and outgoing vessels.

The people grouped on the far left of the frame seem to be getting a large hand-capstan, or *crab*, in position, to draw the hulk onto the beach. There would have needed to be sufficient water under this not only to have enabled it to float free of the sand beneath, but also for the keel to have cleared a wooden breakwater which was located close to the South Pier at this point and built out at a right-angle to it. It looks very much as if that particular point hadn't quite been reached. If it had, surely WRS would have recorded it. The breakwater can be seen in some of the views featured in the **Resort Activity** section—as does the building visible in the middle of the shot, which was an enclosed shelter with seating inside for the comfort and amenity of users of the Pier. The wooden walling running eastwards from it was to protect people sitting on the inner side from the spray caused by heavy seas impacting upon the timbers of the breakwater. Three children wait expectantly near the rowing-boat, while four or five more are playing at the water's edge, on the extreme right of the picture.

25. Ness Point, 1887

The damaged early sea-defences seen here were located at what is still the United Kingdom's most easterly point. The word "Ness" itself derives from OE *næs*, or possibly ON *nes* (given that the Island of Lothingland has a noticeable Scandinavian influence in its place-names), meaning "nose". Something which sticks out, therefore: a shingle promontory, into the North Sea. At one time, the Ness moved small distances to north or south, depending on how wind and tide moved and deposited the coastal sediments—but, eventually, it became fixed by human intervention and remains so today. A similar form of the root-word, *naze,* is to be found in Essex, at Walton on the Naze between Harwich and Clacton, while *ness* features twice more in Suffolk at Benacre, near Kessingland, and further to the south at Orford. The men and boys sitting on the concrete-and-brick part of the defences (together with the person standing)—the smashed remains of timber groynes just visible—give a sense of scale to the image and make it more effective than it would otherwise have been.

Ness Point Lowestoft 1887

In the year 1540, a gun-battery was built at Ness Point (in the cause of coastal defence), with one on either side of it to north and south. All three of these timber-and-earth blockhouses were located much further to the east than can be seen today, as the Denes have receded considerably over the years through the effect of sea-erosion, but the ones flanking that at Ness Point would have aligned roughly with the North Denes Caravan Site and the bottom of Hamilton Road. References to the manufacture of the guns in the Tower of London are to be found in the documentary series, *Letters and Papers, Foreign and Domestic, Henry VIII,* and the three gunners appointed to operate them are named as Nicholas Sendall, James Hayms and Simon Legge, all on a wage of 6d a day. They would, of course, have trained up local men to assist them as and when needed.

26. Ness Point, 1888

Another view of the same location, taken the following year—but from a little further back than its predecessor. No human figures are present, but the sailing drifter, or *dandy*, more than makes up for this. The vessel has all its sails fully set: loose-footed main, boomed mizzen (both with jigger topsails), staysail and large jib—perhaps to enable it to make way in the apparently calm conditions. Or was the photograph perhaps staged? The boat is certainly well inshore, close to the beach—though the water in this shot is slightly higher than in the previous one, as the woodwork of the damaged section of the groyne cannot be seen. It looks as if repair work is in prospect, however, because the wooden framework lying on its side, on the outer part of the structure, is some kind of mechanism for lifting materials or for pile-driving. The drifter's port registration number on the mainsail cannot be read accurately, but it appears to be two digits with the second one a 3. Vessels of the period which might fit are the *Trial* (LT 23), a converter-smack (i.e. one which

Ness Point Lowestoft 1888

both trawled and drifted), the *Golden City* (LT 33), the *Friends* (LT 53), the *Buttercup* (LT 83) and the *Alice* (LT 93)—all four of which were drifters.

In both shots, scrub vegetation can be seen sticking out of the beach, but exactly what it was cannot be given positive identification. There might possibly be marram grass among what is seen near the concrete wall, but the thicker elements would suggest shrubbery of some kind. It is even possible that it was brushwood which had been dug into the beach to help build up the deposits of sand and shingle created by *longshore drift*—the process whereby material was deposited by tidal action and moved from north to south along the whole of this part of the local coastline—as well as in areas much further afield. Obstacles placed in the way of this process, such as groynes or other obstructions, helped to create a build-up of sediments as an addition to what was already there and thus increase the width of the beach—if only as a temporary feature. Removal of the material by winter storms would then be compensated by replacement of what had been taken, when conditions were favourable.

50. Leisure Activity on Gunton Denes

Gunton Denes were an organic (literally), northern extension of Lowestoft Denes: both comprising an extensive area of beach covered with coarse grasses and scrub—the main use of which was to provide rough grazing for livestock and, in Lowestoft's case, serve as large open-air wharf to handle outgoing and incoming cargoes (this was before the harbour was built and extended)—the merchandise being carried between ships and shore in ferry-boats. Fishing-gear was also serviced there, with ample space to lay out nets and ropes, repair sails and carry out sundry other tasks. Strict manorial control was exercised in both Gunton and Lowestoft, and misuse of the area (such as digging ballast, taking rabbits and even pasturing more animals than the stipulated number) was punishable by fines levied in the annual leet court, which adjudicated upon minor disorder and misdemeanour in the community.

Gunton, as a place-name, does not appear in documentation of any kind until the year 1198 (a *Feet of Fines* property transaction) and its name suggests a combination of Scandinavian and Anglo-Saxon elements.

Gunton Denes 1892

This should not come as a surprise, as about half of the place-names in Lothingland Half-hundred show the same characteristics. "Gunni's tun" suggests that a family of Danish origins gave its name to the settlement and there is vestigial landscape evidence available to suggest that it was formed partly from Corton and partly from Lowestoft, with two substantial areas of (largely) coastal heath being parcelled up to create a new community. Using current means of identification, Corton Long Lane to Hubbard's Loke was the northern sector; Hubbards Loke to Station Road (together with the track to the rear of the houses on the north side of Lyndhurst Road), the southern one. The three roads/footways mentioned are all dead straight and that suggests an arbitrary division of land made without reference to individual property-rights or major landmarks requiring deviation of any kind. Boundaries usually take account of pronounced physical features and/or people's landholdings—and these ones, significantly, don't observe that characteristic.

Apart from the uses noted here, in the first paragraph, the other main function of the Denes was to act as protection, for the soft, local, sand-and-clay cliffs, from erosive action by the sea—a service which they still provide. During the second half of the 18th century, as Lowestoft developed its function as a coastal resort and watering-place, the Denes became a place for visitors to perambulate and take the sea air, but the crowds of people in this picture would seem to suggest that something exceptional was happening to draw such numbers. And what could those two tents be, on the extreme left of the picture?

49. Military Encampment on Gunton Denes

Here's the answer: one very small part of the Suffolk Volunteer Corps' annual summer encampment and review by its commanding officer, which had been going on for thirty years or so when this picture was taken. The Lowestoft element of the militia comprised both Rifle Corps (17th Suffolk) and Artillery Corps (1st Suffolk) volunteers, and the review-day itself was treated as a public holiday in the town. The specific location is able to be identified by the presence of the building in the foreground: the *Warren House*, tenemented here into four cottages, but originally one dwelling. It stood not far to the north of Links Road (originally called *Green*—or *Grene*—*Score*, after a family of that name which lived there). It features on a map of the local coastline created in c. 1580, stretching from Pakefield to Gorleston, and was obviously where the warrener

Gunton Denes 1892

once lived—the manorial officer responsible for the general management of the Denes, particularly in the matter of rabbit-breeding and control. A stream of water emerged from the foot of the cliff near this house (and still does) and, during the second half of the 18ᵗʰ century, it powered a water-mill which ground calcined (burned) flint and cattle-bone into powdered form for use as constituents in making Lowestoft soft-paste porcelain—the white clay itself being dug from a pit (or pits) somewhere in the parish of Gunton, in a location still unidentified. An engraving of this event—taken from a drawing produced on 15 July 1865 and viewed from the top of the cliff—shows massed crowds of onlookers on both the Denes and the cliff-face itself (top hats and parasols a-plenty in the foreground), with the *Warren House* cottages plainly visible. The scene is completed with a calm sea, in the distance, showing trading vessels both at anchor and under way, a couple of the old three-masted herring luggers close in (one under sail and one anchored up), and a single steamboat heading for Great Yarmouth.

It is interesting to note that, in the formation of two local units of militia volunteers in Lowestoft (forerunners of the Territorial Army and, therefore, of today's Army Reserve), there was a visible connection with Samuel Morton Peto's expansion of the town itself. *White's Directory of Suffolk* (1872) informs us that the Rifle Volunteers (enrolled in 1860 and numbering 127 men) had a man named J.L. Clemence as second-in-command, holding the rank of captain—the local architect (of London origins) who was responsible for many elements of Peto's various developments. In addition to this, three younger members of the Lucas family held the rank of lieutenant—they, of course, being connected with Lucas Brothers, the building contractors, who were so closely involved in all of the Lowestoft projects and whose employees largely (even totally, it is said) made up the rifle company itself. There is a less obvious parallel to be drawn between Peto and the Artillery Volunteers (a company of eighty men), but their second-in-command (with the rank of lieutenant) was also an architect: W.O. Chambers, who made his own mark upon the town in certain of the buildings he designed. The drill hall of the Artillery Company is still to be seen, in Arnold Street. And a comparatively recent inner link-road joining the top of Old Nelson Street with St. Peter's Street, was named Artillery Way because of its proximity to this very building—passing immediately to the back of it, with the rear end of the building itself reconstructed to form part of the road's boundary wall.

Reference was made (in the caption of the third photograph in this section) as to the more extensive nature of the Denes at one time, and the military survey referred to in the commentary relating to the first image of all gives a width of "forty score tailor's yards". This measures out in modern terms (and staying Imperial, not Metric) as 1,000 yards, though it is not clear whether the Duke of Norfolk was giving the distance to Whaplond Way (Whapload Road) or to the foot of the cliff. Either way, at about 200 yards or more width today, and taken from the roadway, not the cliff-base, it is possible see how much land has been lost to sea erosion in what is now approaching a 500-year period. So far out from the town itself were the three gun batteries located that the Duke expressed concern about an invading force getting in behind them and burning the houses. Thirty-nine years on from his survey, in 1584, Elizabeth I's government was fearful of a Spanish invasion being launched, under the command of the Duke of Alva, from the occupied Netherlands, their forces landing on the Island of Lothingland. This, they would quickly secure, seize Great Yarmouth and then occupy Norwich (the second city in the realm, after London), before driving on towards the capital. A contingency map was drawn up, naming recusant, Roman Catholic gentry in its communities as potentially suspect in loyalty to the Crown, and an assessment was made of the area's capacity to feed an army. A muster was also taken of the men in each parish able to fight and of the stock of arms available there, which reads a little like a Tudor "Dad's Army" in the number of aging males named—the Latin word *senex* revealing this. In the event, the Spanish Armada sailed four years later, from the home country—but that is another story.

TOWN AND SURROUNDS

17. Lighthouse Score (al. Lighthouse Hill)

Lowestoft Highlight

The title used by WRS is negated, to a certain degree, by the lighthouse itself being hard to detect in the top right-hand corner of the photograph—hence the heading chosen by the writer. Lowestoft had eleven scores during the 19th and 20th centuries, three of them being for vehicle use (Gunton—al. The Ravine—Cart, and Rant) and eight as footways—one of the latter (Frost's Alley) being no longer wholly in existence. The word *score* itself derives from ON *skora*, meaning "to cut" or "to incise", and the scores themselves were originally surface-water runnels down the face of the soft, clay cliff-line, which were used by people to access and depart from the Denes. Once the Lowestoft community had relocated itself from the settlement's original site (somewhere in the north-eastern sector of what is now the municipal cemetery between Normanston Drive and Rotterdam Road) onto a new cliff-top location, during the first half of the 14th century, these improvised trackways underwent a process of management. Flanking and protective walls were constructed and steps and paving introduced.

The town's first pair of *leading lights* appeared down on the beach in 1609, placed there with the permission of Trinity House to assist safe passage through the offshore sandbanks (via the Stanford Channel) into safe anchorage. This was done by picking up the alignment of the two markers, out at sea, and sailing straight towards them. It was the second navigational aid of its kind—the first having been erected at Caister in 1607 to provide a similar service for Great Yarmouth. In 1628, John Wild (mariner and merchant) was authorised by Trinity House to build a "high lighthouse" (with which the lower one would align) towards the top of Mariner's Score, on its northern side. This remained in operation until 1676, when the fire-risk to nearby houses, caused by sparks issuing from its coal- or wood-burning brazier, resulted in its being closed down and superseded by a replacement about a quarter of a mile to the north—built on a piece of manorial waste-ground. Samuel Pepys, in his capacity as Master of Trinity House, gave the order for its construction and the site is still in use today. The building seen, however (just visible in the photograph, here), with its accompanying cottages, was erected in 1873—and no lighthouse-keepers have lived in the houses since the electrified light went automatic in 1970. The shadowy building seen behind the trees on the slope of the cliff is the storage facility provided for the fuel-oil, and other equipment, used to power the light up until 1938 when electricity was first introduced.

The photograph's foreground is dominated by the front gardens (and one shed!) belonging to a row of unseen, early 18th century cottages. These were demolished during the 1930s and the space re-developed for local authority housing. The left-hand mid-space shows part of *The Shoals* net-store complex, owned by J.V. Breach—member of one of the many families who came into Lowestoft from fishing-stations in Kent and Sussex during the second half of the 19th century, when the local East Anglian fishing industry was booming. He lived on Whapload Road, next to his work-place, and *Hastings House* was the name of his dwelling. Part of these distinctive industrial premises, with their imaginative brick-and-flint construction, had already undergone demolition, before the rest was fortunately saved and converted to modern domestic living accommodation.

22. The Ravine & Its Bridge

Gunton Score was re-named "The Ravine" at some point during the 19th century—possibly to coincide with the opening of Belle Vue Park (1874), which occupied land formerly functioning as the town's North Common—one of seven areas of manorial waste dating from the medieval period (the others being the Denes, Goose or Fair Green, Church Green, Skamacre Heath, Drake's Heath and the South Common). It was part of the parish boundary between Lowestoft and its neighbour to the north and the re-naming was possibly carried out to raise the profile of the area and create a new image. According to local reports of the time, the North Common had become a gathering-place for those disposed to idleness and misdemeanour, and a civic scheme was put in place to turn it into a place of polite resort and amenity. Gunton Score, then, was consigned to memory and "The Ravine" became its successor—a name suggestive of naturalistic and romantic landscape.

An even earlier name than "Gunton Score" had far more sinister overtones, for the trackway had once been known as "Gallows Score" (and "Hangman's Hill"), and it is possible that a place of execution (or a gibbet) had once stood on this bleak piece of heath, beyond the edge of town, with "runs" for livestock and other tracks crossing and passing it. During the 13th and 14th centuries, Lowestoft had shared the governance of Lothingland Half-hundred with Gorleston (the manorial hub), with right of gaol and stocks, and right of gallows could also have been included. As we see it here, looking westwards up the slope, Belle Vue Park is on the left and North Parade on the right, with the bridge linking them together. It was the gift of William

Youngman (brewer), the town's first mayor following its incorporation in 1885, and it opened in the year 1887—Queen Victoria's Golden Jubilee. It was a mere youngster, therefore, when WRS set up his tripod and snapped it.

Today, he would be standing on a metalled surface, with cars and vans heading down towards him—the roadway being a vehicular, one-way route down to the North Denes and Whapload Road, with neighbouring Cart Score to the south taking traffic in the opposite direction, upwards. William Youngman's company (Youngman & Preston Ltd.) produced beer at the Eagle Brewery, north side of Rant Score at its junction with Whapload Road, and he himself lived at No. 63 High Street. Belle Vue Park remains, to this day, a pleasant public garden, and it has national significance through its containing the official memorial to men of the Royal Naval Patrol Service killed on active duty during the Second World War—Lowestoft being the chief base of this front-line operation, manned by RNR fishermen. A total of 2,835 names are recorded on it.

Ravine Bridge, Lowestoft

5. 16 Marine Parade

Marine Parade Lowestoft

William Smith Snr., father of WRS, probably retired from corn-milling at Dickleburgh in 1881, when he was sixty-nine years of age, moving into 16 Marine Parade (the middle house of the three shown here) with his third wife, Sarah. The property had belonged to her since 1868, and their marriage and its arrangements were discussed earlier in the **Preface**. The Census Return of 1891 shows that William's daughter Eliza (aged forty-six years) was acting as his housekeeper (he was three times widowed by then) and that Rosa Hubbard, aged twenty-four, was a live-in domestic servant and cook. This terrace of three-storey dwellings, with basements below (forty-eight units in all, originally—which later became fifty), was part of Samuel Morton Peto's resort development of the late 1840s to mid 1850s and the dwellings (built 1852-5) were described at the time of construction as "excellent second-rate houses"—this, by way of contrast with the large, detached *villas* which occupied the sea-front itself and prevented their lesser neighbours from having a fully direct view of the ocean. Nevertheless, the latter were substantial and comfortable places to live—either on a seasonal or permanent basis—and they were purchased by people who were financially well off.

The terrace was built by Lucas Brothers and the Lowestoft Marine Parade Building Society was formed on 1 September 1850 to manage sale of the properties (in advance of their construction), with Thomas Lucas in control. The houses were sold in the form of individual shares held in the building society, with forty-eight of these being available. Mortgage arrangements were available to those people wishing to use this method of buying one. All of the houses were leasehold, with an annual ground rent of £2 per annum payable to Samuel Morton Peto—this practice being established by a indenture of 15 April 1851. The first owner of No. 16 was Arthur Dalrymple Esq. of Norwich, who purchased it on 29 December 1855 for the sum of £185 2s 8d, with the deed of sale describing the process as being the transfer of Share No. 16 from Mr. Thomas Lucas to him.

It is hard to be completely accurate in converting sums of money from earlier times into modern values, but around £15,000 in today's terms would not be too far out. At the time, such a payment would have been within the means of people who formed what may be described as the "middling level of society" involved in business, commerce and professional activity of different kinds. Dalrymple was a Norwich lawyer, son of the renowned surgeon William Dalrymple. He was a bibliophile and lover of the arts and, when he died in 1868, eleven large folios of drawings, engravings, photographs and manuscript notes on local worthies was acquired by Jeremiah James Colman, the Norwich mustard manufacturer. They remain an important part of the Colman Library collection, in the stewardship of Norfolk County Council.

A Colman connection is also to be found with regard to No. 8 Marine Parade, which was bought from new by James Colman, mustard manufacturer of Stoke Holy Cross in Norfolk, and passed to his son, the famous Jeremiah James, on his death in 1854. The company moved to Carrow Works, in Norwich, in 1856 and expanded its operation greatly. Jeremiah James Colman moved to Corton in 1869, acquiring a cliff-top residence called *The Clyffe*, which he extended considerably, and he lived there until his death in 1898. At some point, after coming to Corton, he bought a grander seaside residence at No. 20 Wellington Esplanade (al. Terrace) and held that for a number of years, passing No. 8 over to his mother. She retained the property up to her death in September 1898 (three days before that of her son). Whether or not she lived there all year is not known, but *Huke's Lowestoft Directory* (1892) records her occupancy also. Another notable presence in the row, just two doors away from William Smith Snr., was that of local architect J.L. Clemence at No. 14—the local "man on the ground" for Samuel Morton Peto, who designed the Marine Parade terrace itself as well as many other buildings forming part of Lowestoft's expansion. And not just in the southern resort-area, but in other parts of town as well. Among the many things he was responsible for was the *Harbour Village* (to the north of the Inner Harbour), which consisted of three spacious roads named Selby Street, Clemence Street and Stevens Street, whose distinctive terraced houses still take the eye today.

Wellington Esplanade was (and is) a monumental terrace—Grade II listed and often attributed to Peto's London architect, John Thomas (but with features suggesting more of an input from J.L. Clemence)—situated about 400 yards further to the north of Marine Parade and consisting of twenty-four units. But what a difference in scale: a central block of six four-storey dwellings, with two flanking blocks of seven three-storey ones, and terminating blocks of two four-storey units at either end—all with basements! And not only that, but an unimpeded view of the sea, provided by an elegant, open, communal garden-space, accessed by locked gates and separated from the houses by the road to Pakefield interposing. Even today, in spite of all the changes that have taken place, Wellington Esplanade still has a statement to make about the scale and imposing presence of "high-end" Victorian seaside architecture.

All of Samuel Morton Peto's Lowestoft development was carried out using bricks made at Somerleyton, where he had taken up residence in 1844. He had purchased the local brickworks there in 1849, from the Green family, turning it over soon afterwards to Charles and Thomas Lucas of Lowestoft (both of London origins, with the former also having operated in Norwich) and following this up with a twenty-one year lease agreement in 1854. The expansion of the town was reflected in that of the Somerleyton operation itself. Both red and white bricks were turned out in large numbers (Marine Parade being built of whites and Wellington Esplanade a blend of the two) and were landed for use in the Lucas Bros. joinery-works yard on the south side of Lowestoft Inner Harbour—brought there by wherry from Somerleyton Staithe and possibly also by rail from its station. This yard, and its wharf, was located on the bend in Belvedere Road (later to become the site of C. & E. Morton's food-canning factory), named after the Lucas Bros. base in Belvedere Road, Lambeth—the company opening up there in 1852, after having had an office in The Strand for a year or two previously.

Before leaving No. 16 Marine Parade itself, certain things in the photograph are worth commenting on. The house is the one in the middle of the shot and it has had its hedge cut to a level just above the top of the metal fence—whereas the one to the left is very low (perhaps recently planted), which allows the top of the basement window to be seen. The creeper on the facade is not that old, reaching only as high as the top of the ground-floor level—contrasting with the one next door, which has gone one storey higher, albeit cut back in similar fashion. Comparisons of both may be made with the dwelling on the far right, where the vegetation has been well and truly allowed to get a hold. Close inspection of the houses shows that the front-gates of Nos. 16 & 17 have a roundel in the middle, with crossed diagonal bars passing through—creating a pleasing appearance, which sits well with the overall design of the fencing itself.

Partially drawn Venetian blinds are visible in the downstairs windows of all three dwellings shown here *in toto*, and, if the ground-floor bay of No. 16 is studied closely, WRS's father and sister Eliza can be seen looking out at him taking the photograph—a large pot-plant standing between them. All in all, a lovely family touch, which adds greatly to the effect this view has on anyone knowing the full significance of those faces at the window. No. 15's window has its own face, too: that of a young boy, looking out himself, but probably not at the photographer. The window of No. 17 has no human presence, but there are plants and other things on the windowsill and what looks like the best part of a birdcage hanging down. A canary, perhaps, or a goldfinch—favourite feathered captives of the time.

48. W.E. Gladstone's Arrival (17 May 1890)

Continuing from the previous image, we remain with a Colman family connection because Mr. Gladstone's arrival at Lowestoft Railway Station during the afternoon of Saturday, 17 May 1890, was the result of him not coming to the town itself *per se*, but using a train from Norwich in order to visit Jeremiah James Colman at his home in Corton. The "Grand Old Man" was eighty years old and in between his third and fourth terms of office as Prime Minister (the latter a record for any British premier). The *Norfolk Chronicle* reported on how he had addressed a Liberal and Radical gathering at the Agricultural Hall in Norwich on the Friday evening— having been met earlier on his arrival at Thorpe Station by J.J. Colman and hosted at *Carrow Abbey*—and then spent the night at the home of a supporter (Henry Birkbeck) in Stoke Holy Cross, before leaving for Lowestoft the following afternoon.

Notice of his arrival there travelled far beyond the attention of just the local press, for the *South Wales Daily News* described how he was presented with an illuminated address on the Railway Station's platform by Liberal Party supporters and addressed the company gathered there. It also gave an account of how the route from Lowestoft to Corton was lined with people, as well as giving some details of his stay at *The Clyffe*. It may have been an exaggeration to have described the roadway as being thronged for the whole of the three-mile distance, but the crowds in Lowestoft were certainly out in force. The view presented here in WRS's photograph shows Mr. and Mrs. Gladstone sitting in their carriage (facing the camera), under police escort, accompanied by their third son, Henry, and his wife—guests also of the Colmans. The shot was taken from a first-floor window in No. 34 London Road North—a shop-premises belonging to Cubitt Bros. (tobacconists, hairdressers & photographers), with whom WRS obviously had a commercial or professional connection. The site today is occupied by the HSBC Bank.

The doorway seen on the immediate left of the picture (on the other side of Beach Road) is that of Henry Tuttle's *Bon Marche* drapery & general furnishings shop, which eventually grew into the town's largest department store—occupying the whole of the space between Beach Road and Waveney Road. Its successor now gives access to *The Joseph Conrad* public house. The view down Denmark Road, along which everyone is processing from the Railway Station is a revelation: fine Victorian residences, with neat, well-tended front gardens and a substantial, well-proportioned commercial premises at the end, nearest the camera. This was the *Railway Café*, a Temperance place-of-refreshment, providing something different from what was on sale in the town's many licensed establishments. The view down Bevan Street, on the right of the picture, shows that it is almost deserted. Perhaps even the customary frequenters of the *Stone Cottage* tavern, seen in the distance down at the junction with Tonning Street (its gothic ground-floor doorway and windows clearly seen) had left their usual haunt to join the crowds. There is a considerable social mix of people on show, with a noticeable element of fishermen among them, some following the equipage, with another company

Mr. Gladstone at Lowestoft

assembled on the right of the picture. A number of these can be seen to be wearing either their working *gansies* or their *tan jumpers* (calico slops dyed with a red-ochre mixture used to preserve ships' sails) with their headgear revealing their status on board: caps for everyone up to the rank of mate, bowler-hats for skippers. The one thing largely missing from the crowd is any substantial female presence—the only obvious sign of women being there are the ones standing below where WRS took his picture and a few, with children, at the end of Bevan Street. Late Victorian politics was very much a man's world—and some people, today, would argue that it still is!

The Gladstone party's stay at *The Clyffe*, Corton, lasted until Tuesday, 20 May, when the company returned to London. Mr. Gladstone knew Jeremiah James Colman well, for the latter had served as one of the two Norwich MPs (as a Liberal member) from 1871—eventually ending his parliamentary career in 1895. His daughter, Helen, in her privately published *Jeremiah James Colman: A Memoir* (1905) pp. 403-5, used notes her mother had made, as part of a personal record of the visit, recalling a number of the dinner-time conversations which took place during Gladstone's time in the house. Forty-eight topics are listed altogether, covering a wide range of subject-areas: Biblical matters, politics and political figures, the arts, science, history, sporting activities and other things. Within a local context, Lowestoft porcelain is mentioned, as is the work of John Crome the Elder of the Norwich School of Artists, and round-tower churches are also referred to. It is not revealed whether or not Gladstone left any mustard on his plate, having eaten his meal—for that practice, over the whole of the country, was how (or so Jeremiah James Colman claimed) the family fortune had been made!

The "Grand Old Man" visited the Colmans again just over a year later, in June 1891, as part of a recovery process from a severe bout of influenza—but that is not part of this particular story.

52. Bridge Scene

The album-title given by WRS to this shot has no indication whatsoever of what had caused such a concourse of people on and around the first harbour bridge (in operation 1830-97)—the water in the channel beneath it showing that the tide is low, judging by the reflected "sun-spots' on its surface. The crowd is seen to be moving in both directions and the time of day would appear to be round about noon, if the size and alignment of people's shadows is anything to go by. The Harbour Master's and Deputy's dwellings are prominent in the middle of the picture, as is the thatched ice-house and its two-way gantry used for taking in consignments of ice and for loading the ice-wherries which transferred ice to the trawlers for preserving catches at sea. To begin with, ice was cut from local marshes and stretches of water during the winter, once frozen over, and then kept in the insulated brick building for as long as it was possible to make it last. The broad at Oulton was a major source, of course, as were the Norfolk Broads, but it wasn't long before the largest supplies of all were brought in by ship from the Norwegian fjords. Local waters just couldn't produce enough for what was needed when the fishing industry rapidly expanded after Samuel Morton Peto had improved the harbour works and brought the railway to Lowestoft. Eventually, in 1898, the East Anglian Ice Company Ltd. built a factory to manufacture the product at a site on Riverside Road, on the south side of the Inner Harbour, and this remained in operation until it was replaced in 1962 by one at the back of the Fish Market area, close to Battery Green Road. With the collapse of the Lowestoft fishing industry, this building has stood empty and derelict for many years and serves mainly, now, to provide a nesting place for the most easterly colony of kittiwakes in the UK.

The gathering of people seen here may have been due to a public holiday of some kind (though WRS does annotate one of his other photographs "Lowestoft Beach, Whit Monday"—used in the **Resort Activity** section), or it might have been Regatta Day in late August. But, there again, "Regatta Day" is specifically referred to in two of the images featured in **Harbour Views**, so the matter remains unresolved. Only the gentleman in the right-of-centre foreground is seen wearing a top-coat of any kind—and that's undone and hanging loosely. All the other men, who are clearly visible, are jacketed and the women do not seem to be heavily attired either. Spring or summer, then, but with no easy means of identifying the occasion. A ladder can be seen propped against the right-hand one of a pair of gas-lamps located in the foreground, so presumably some kind of maintenance or repair work is to be carried out at some point—but perhaps not while the crowds swarm! David Boxall, co-author with his wife, Jennifer, of Volume 1, has suggested that if WRS was doing office work of some kind in his brother-in-law's corn-milling business in Harleston (remember that he was given the title of "clerk" in the 1881 Canadian census return), he might therefore have visited Lowestoft at weekends. That is possible, of course—yet, at the same time, this seems to have been a particularly busy one. And everyone crossing the bridge from south to north is being told to KEEP TO THE RIGHT, away from the edge of the bridge channel, by a painted notice placed on the ground.

The iron bridge seen here was opened manually, on either side, whereby each of the two sections (which met in the middle) split from the other and swung inwards in opposite directions, thus clearing the channel for shipping to enter or leave the Inner Harbour. The northern one's turning-space can be seen on the left-hand side of the picture and the southern one's safety barrier (pushed across to close the gap when the bridge was open) is clearly visible behind the advertisement board—a wheelbarrow standing next to it. Its companion on the other side of the water can also be seen, in front of the canopied extension to the cottages. And thus did "bridgers" come to be part of Lowestoft's folklore: the mechanical process which regularly cut the town in half and brought all land-based movement to a halt, but allowed seaborne traffic to have free way.

In 1897, a new swing bridge replaced the one seen here: a single section, which swung to rest its length against the northern wall of the bridge-channel, with sufficient space left for shipping to pass. It jammed in the open position in January 1969, causing severe disruption over the town as a whole. A temporary footbridge was quickly put in place to allow pedestrians, cyclists and motorbike-riders to cross the water, sliding back periodically to allow ships to pass, and a ferry service also operated. But these could do nothing

Lowestoft

to cater for cars, vans and lorries (all of which had to make a detour through Oulton Broad, whether heading north or south) so a retractable bridge was built just to the west of the disabled one. Nothing could be done to repair the latter, which was dismantled, removed and replaced by the double-leaf bascule in use today—a process lasting two years or more. Opening in 1972, that too has had its problems over the years, and the third crossing (to pass over the Inner Harbour between Riverside Road on the south and the junction of Denmark Road-Rotterdam Road-Peto Way on the north)—its construction having been given final approval—can't come soon enough.

24. Mutford Lock

Mutford Lock

This shot must have been taken from near the northern edge of Lake Lothing's western extremity (probably from wooden staging located there). The meeting-point of this stretch of brackish water with the broad at Oulton had, for centuries, been a fording-point, with the former's periodic tidal flow over the shingle-bar at Lowestoft (located where the bridge now is) controlled by an earthen dam over which the highway passed. This feature is described by the writer, Thomas Baskerville, when he visited Lowestoft in 1677, taking the road from Beccles as his approach. He refers to it as "a dam of earth between 10 and 20 yards broad, secured on the right hand seaward with piles of wood to break the fury of the waves." The "piles", of course, were hardwood stakes (probably oak) driven into the bed of the lake, not heaps of timber. This reinforcement had been put in place to counter the effect of high tides, but it had no means of withstanding surges when they occurred—such as that of January 1607, which carried away both the Lowestoft bar and the earthen dam and flooded the River Waveney's marshes up as far as Bungay—to say nothing of swamping the grazing-lands of the Chet and Yare, at Loddon and Langley! Another occurred in December 1717 and, following this, a wooden bridge was put in place to carry the roadway and make it less vulnerable to inundation—superseded by a replacement of sturdier brick-build in 1760.

The term "Mutford" has nothing to do with the local village of that name, nor is it a variant of "mud ford" in reference to the former dam separating the two lagoons. Both roots of the word are OE *(ge)mōt* and *ford*, meaning "the ford where meetings are held". This identifies the place, most probably, as the ancient, Anglo-Saxon point of assembly for the two half-hundreds of Lothingland and Mutford, where the monthly courts of enquiry and adjudication were held—a proposition reinforced by documentation surviving from the late 16th and early 17th centuries: specifically, the records (covering the years 1590-1612) of a six-monthly manorial court known as the *tourn,* which dealt with matters of misdemeanour and irregularity infringing the laws of both hundredal jurisdictions. This met in a building located close to the crossing-place, more or less on the elevated ground where the present-day *Commodore* public house stands. A study of both Lake Lothing and the adjacent broad suggests that their alignment with each other shows them to have been the Waveney's outlet to the sea at some point in the past—though what forced the river to divert northwards and eventually flow into Breydon Water, almost next to the Yare, is not known. Both stretches of water were greatly extended in area by the digging of peat, from around the edges, during the medieval and early modern periods. Lowestoft's parish registers give evidence of this, in the burial entry of the wife of John Browne (17 February 1605), the latter being described as a *flag-graver*. The area of Lake Lothing nearest to the broad has traditionally been referred as "the salt side" (and it does have a saline content and is tidal), but a Lowestoft manorial roll of 1618, which lists practically every piece of land and every building in the parish, refers to the mere as "the Fresh Water"—probably to contrast it with the sea, from which it was separated by the shingle bar.

The scene captured here by WRS focuses on the lock, which gave the location its name, and on the buildings situated close by. As was mentioned earlier, in the Introduction, it was constructed as part of William Cubitt's harbour works at Lowestoft (1827-30) and his associated scheme to create an alternative navigation to Norwich to rival that provided by Great Yarmouth. The lock can be seen to the left of centre, with people standing on the bridge above and with the expanse of Oulton's broad lying beyond. The group of buildings, centre-right, stand on land occupied today by the *Wherry Hotel*—its precursor among them. An advertisement by the latter's proprietor, George Mason, in *White's Directory of Suffolk* (1872) says that "THIS DELIGHTFUL SPOT SHOULD BE VISITED by all coming to the neighbourhood. Every ACCOMMODATION is provided for FISHING and BOATING, including Fishing Tackle and Bait; and the Waters are well stocked with Fish. A spacious SALOON faces the Broad, over which is a Commodious BALCONY, affording a splendid View of the whole extent of the Water. The Grounds are Ornamentally Laid Out, and, together with a BOWLING GREEN, also face the Broad. SITTING ROOM and BED ROOM Accommodation for permanent or casual Visitors is available, at very reasonable charges." Who, at the time, could resist such delights!

Significantly, perhaps, the advertisement does not mention the proximity of a lime-kiln, which can be seen on the far right of the photograph—a wherry itself moored against the quay. These distinctive and iconic vessels of the local waterways carried all kinds of cargo (grain, malt, hay, timber, bricks and coal)—though, in this case, it would have been mined chalk in one direction and quick-lime in the other. *White's Directory* informs the reader that the kiln belonged to John Knights Jnr. (bricklayer and lime-burner) and that a Mrs. Maria Knights (probably his mother) was a lime merchant—a neat little family business—though one which must have detracted from the advertised delights of the nearby hotel—the balcony of which can just be seen on the one-storey saloon extension, on the left-hand side of the main building.

6. Ready for the Off, Carlton Colville

It may not have gone unnoticed that there was no direct reference to Oulton Broad in the comments relating to the previous picture. This was because nowhere of that name existed at the time and because the broad itself belonged as much to Carlton Colville as to Oulton. Oulton Broad, the place, was created as a civil parish in 1904 and followed as an ecclesiastical one as late as 1931. Though St. Mark's Church had been built during 1883-4, it originally functioned as a chapel-of-ease to the parish church of St. Peter, Carlton Colville, serving the needs of the community which had grown up in the Mutford Bridge area on the back of the Lowestoft-Norwich Navigation, first of all, and then on the development of the railway and harbour works at Lowestoft carried out by Samuel Morton Peto. Oulton Broad was created from land situated in Carlton Colville and Oulton itself, with the former parish (at 2,804 acres) being the largest one in the Hundred of Mutford and Lothingland—the two former half-hundreds having been made into one, for Poor Law purposes, in 1763.

Not only did Carlton Colville occupy the whole of the southern edge of the broad, but most of that adjoining Lake Lothing also—its great East Heath occupying much of the area taken up today by Bridge Road and Beccles Road, Victoria Road, Waveney Drive and all the associated lesser roads and housing to the east and south of these. What is now known as Oulton Broad South railway station was originally known as Carlton Station (the first one out of Lowestoft, on Peto's line to Ipswich) and elderly acquaintances of the

Mr. Patrick's Carlton

writer, native to the village, were still calling it that during the 1970s! Originally called simply Carlton (Latinised as *Carletuna* and *Karletuna* in the Domesday Survey), the name derives either from OScand *Karla* (a personal name) or OE *ceorl* meaning "a freeman", with the second element being OE *tun* meaning "village" or "settlement". The Colville was added during the early 13th century, when the de Coleville family (incomers from Coleville-sur-Mer, in Normandy, accompanying Duke William in 1066) became lords of the manor for a time.

But who was Mr. Patrick? Presumably, the heavily bearded man on the right, with the walking stick and terrier. And if this is the case, what was his connection with WRS? Volume I of the latter's work reveals part of an answer in its **Character List**, on p. 81, where it is recorded that his youngest brother Horace (born in 1857) married a woman named Mary Marston Patrick. Further investigation has revealed that the wedding took place in St. Peter's Church, Carlton Colville, on 24 June 1885, and the couple must have left for Canada shortly afterwards, as a son (Ivan) was born there, in Montreal, in 1886. This move abroad parallels that of WRS and his wife, as referred to in the **Preface**, but for a much shorter period of time, because Ivan and Mary were back and living in Lowestoft by 1891. And so, a family link gives a reason for WRS to be present at Mr. Patrick's house—though there is no way of knowing exactly what this was.

Mary Patrick herself had been born in Kettleburgh, Suffolk, in 1861 and was baptised in the parish church there on 11 May. This makes her twenty-four years of age on her wedding-day and thirty in 1891, when she and her husband had returned to Lowestoft—surely far too young for her to be the woman in the photograph, seated in the trap. Perhaps it is Harriet, Mr. Patrick's wife (née Girling), waiting for him to join her in the vehicle and take the reins. The groom or farmhand holding the pony's bridle faces the camera as directly as his employers, his buttoned leather gaiters typical working-wear of the time and with the foot-scraper on the doorstep behind him reminding us of just how much mud boots and shoes could pick up in wet weather—to say nothing of what else might be lying underfoot to get picked up in farmyards!

And William Kenney Patrick was a farmer, born at Grimston in Norfolk c. 1826 (near King's Lynn), but someone who spent most of his adult working-life in Suffolk—in two particular areas: the Glemham-Woodbridge one, to begin with, followed by twenty years or more in the Lowestoft-Beccles locality. He moved from place to place on the typical short-term farm tenancies of the period—his movements detectable in Census Returns and other documentation. He first turns up at Great Glemham in 1859 in a *Poll Book & Electoral Register* collection, while two years later the 1861 Census finds him in nearby Kettleburgh. In 1872, *White's Directory of Suffolk* lists him as resident at *Grove Farm*, Little Bealings (near Woodbridge), and by 1881 the Census of that year places him at *White House Farm,* Flixton (near Lowestoft), a unit of 200 acres employing eight men and a boy. By 1891, he had retired to No. 139 Station Road, Beccles—so WRS must have caught him at Carlton Colville between Flixton and there, not long before he moved—and 1901 saw him established at 36 Lorne Park Road, in Kirkley. He obviously moved back to his native North-west Norfolk, eventually, and his death is recorded in probate material as occurring on 6 April 1916 at King's Lynn.

His house, shown here in the photograph, with an older barn to the side, is of comparatively modern construction by comparison and probably of mid-19th century origins. The first-floor is built of white brick—often preferred to red as being suggestive of higher quality and fashionable at the time—while the ground-floor level has the appearance of being constructed of stone, with its geometric slabs having deeply-raked joints to suggest *banded rustication*. However, it may well be appearance only, with the whole façade being made of finely worked plaster *stucco* applied to underlying brickwork and made to look like stone. Whatever the case, the masonry is of good quality, with the finely shaped cornice of the doorway being particularly notable. The fenestration is well proportioned, with recessed sash windows and stone (or simulated stone) surrounds, and the whole combination of the features seen on the façade produces an air of pleasing restraint in a building that is both substantial and easy on the eye. Although not seen in full, it looks very similar in appearance to *Carlton Hall*.

16. Kessingland Cliff

This section began with an image of a cliff and it ends with one five miles or more to the south. But whereas the area of cliff photographed at Lowestoft (with Lighthouse Score traversing it) showed buildings on the lower sections and trees planted on its face, the picture seen here is of the raw item—untouched by human intervention. The whole of the cliff at Lowestoft had been terraced from end to end during the first half of the 14th century, when the town changed its location—work, at the time, of a monumental nature which served to make the cliff-face usable and form the staged burgage-plots of the houses which stood along the east side of the High Street. The first terrace below the dwellings provided garden-areas and, the lower two, spaces for buildings connected largely with maritime pursuits: stables, storage sheds, salt-houses, fish-houses (for curing the catches) and net-stores.

Kessingland cliff.

There is no such development discernible in this image. The face of the cliff, somewhere to the north of Kessingland village, is largely composed of glacial sand and clay, the stratigraphy of which is clearly visible, with the topsoil layer noticeably darker than the underlying material. Its vulnerability to the erosive action of wind, weather and the sea is also plain to see and, since the end of the 18th century, something like 300 yards or more of cliff-line has been lost to the sea along this stretch of coast. There was a small, nucleated area of habitation at Kessingland in the vicinity of the parish church, from early times, but with a much wider pattern of dispersed settlement in evidence across the whole of the parish. Farmsteads and cottages stood in isolation and a triangular green (cut through by a modern bypass) was located within the overall pattern of a common-field system of agriculture.

The old, medieval landscape is vestigial, and still detectable in places, but Kessingland (as seen today) is largely the result of 19th century development along the High Street and Church Road, together with another part of the village which grew up close to the sea at the lower end of Church Road at about the same time. Building development during the second half of the 20th century, between Field Lane and Church Road increased the size of the community considerably and the Kessingland of today is not the one which WRS would have seen. As might be expected of any coastal settlement, the village's main occupations at one time were farming and fishing—the latter being of the *longshore* variety, with small boats working directly off the beach and with the fishermen and their families living in close proximity to the sea. The community created in this area was therefore analogous, in many ways, to that of the "Beach Village" at Lowestoft—and it wasn't the only connection between Kessingland and its much larger neighbour.

During the late Victorian and the Edwardian periods (the latter, really, just an extension of its predecessor), as the Lowestoft herring trade grew in capacity, a number of Kessingland men became involved in its expansion as leading boat-owners. One of them, George ("Mouse") Catchpole, had the first steam drifter of all built in 1897 (the *Consolation*, LT 718), which was said to have been so-named because of it retaining its mainmast and sail (as well as the mizzen)—thereby assuring it the consolation of wind-power if, and when, steam-propulsion failed! In the event, all subsequent steam drifters retained the mainmast (renamed foremast), with the gaff being used as a boom or derrick when landing herrings. And diesel craft continued the practice when they eventually superseded steam. Kessingland itself prospered so greatly on the back of the "silver darlings" that it became known locally as "Klondyke"—reputedly the richest village in the kingdom—its wealth comparable with that made by prospectors during the Yukon "gold-rush" of the 1890s. A similar claim was also made at one time for Caister, regarding its own advantageous relationship with Great Yarmouth.

WRS's visit to Kessingland, therefore, was made at just about the time the village was approaching its high-point in terms of affluence (though not, it has to be said, for everyone) and the photograph he took concentrates solely on a section of its cliff-face. Well not quite solely, because the leather Gladstone bag sitting on the beach, nearest the camera (surely, his own), and the terrier behind it, serve to give some kind of perspective to the shot. At first glance, the dog looks rather like the one in the previous image, but the markings on its head show that it isn't. It is, in fact, WRS's own animal, which features in Volume I, p. 77, curled up on a *chaise longue* in a room inside *Mill House* at Harleston. It obviously accompanied its master on his trips to Lowestoft. But how did they both get out to Kessingland with Gladstone bag (presumably containing camera and glass-plates) and tripod? Was transport from the town arranged? Or were they perhaps taken there in William Kenney Patrick's trap?

HARVEST OF THE SEA

7. Sailing Drifter & Tug

Lowestoft from Pier

This scene of tranquillity was taken from the South Pier—almost certainly at its seaward extremity. The calm surface of the sea has almost been lost in the processing of the print and the fine line of the horizon is practically indiscernible. A single-funnel steam-tug is seen well astern of the sailing drifter as they both head into port. The Great Eastern Railway Company had a number of the steam-tugs based at Lowestoft, over the years, after it had taken up the running of the port and the associated rail links with Norwich and Ipswich (in 1862) following Samuel Morton Peto relinquishing his interests. Among their tasks was the towing of craft out of (and sometimes into) the harbour in adverse weather and tidal conditions. These "workhorses" often feature in photographs and, among them, were vessels named *Imperial, May* and *Powerful* (single funnel and steam-paddle driven), *Despatch* and *Rainbow* (twin funnel and steam-paddle), and *Resolute* (single funnel and screw).

The sailing drifter shown here was named the *Alert* (LT 551) and she was a typical vessel of her time, often referred to as a *dandy* because of her ketch- or gaff-rig (also known as *dandy-rig*). This sail-pattern had been progressively adopted during the 1870s, replacing the old lugsail one, its cut-away quadrilateral main and mizzen sails being easier to handle than their large, square predecessors. However, even when no more two-masted *luggers* were left in the Lowestoft fishing-fleet, there was still a tendency for people to use that term to describe their successors! The boat has topsails (or *tops'ls*) set on both masts and a large jib out on the bowsprit, to catch as much wind as possible—but, even so, the canvas is hardly billowing! Both the *loose-footed* mainsail and the mizzen have *bonnets* laced to them, at the foot: extra lengths of canvas put in place to create a greater area for the wind to work on. Their lines of attachment are plain to see.

When WRS took this photograph (loosely, round about 1890), steam power had not yet reached the Lowestoft fishing fleet—except in the matter of capstans. The engineering firm of Elliott & Garrood, of Beccles, fitted the first one it produced into a sailing drifter called the *Beaconsfield* (LT 156) in 1884, and its efficiency and space-saving capacity on deck (compared with hand-capstans) revolutionised the task of hauling nets— both drifting-gear and trawls. Between the 1880s and 1960s, Elliott's (as they were often known locally) fitted over 7,000 steam capstans into British and European fishing craft—a remarkable achievement by the company and a tribute to the effectiveness of its invention. Steam propulsion of fishing-craft themselves arrived over a decade later and reference was made (in comments relating to the last picture in the previous section) to the first steam herring-drifter being built in 1897—and it was an innovation which soon caught on because of the advantages it had over sail.

At eighty feet or so long, a steam vessel was twenty feet or more longer than its sailing counterpart, which meant that it could carry more nets and catch more fish. It could also travel more quickly to and from the fishing-grounds, which speeded up the fishing operation itself and made this more cost-effective. And it was less affected by adverse weather conditions, while at sea, and did not have to be towed out of harbour by a GER tug if there was too little wind or if it was blowing from the wrong direction. The *Consolation* (LT 718) was laid down and launched in 1897, as has been said. By 1903, *Flood's Lowestoft Port Directory* lists 169 sailing drifters in Lowestoft, 234 sailing trawlers (or *smacks*), 4 converter-smacks (which carried out both kinds of fishing) and 69 steam drifters (including the *Consolation*). In 1911—using *Olsen's Fisherman's Nautical Almanack* of that year and the writer's own records— the number of steam drifters and drifter-trawlers (the latter being able to work all year round and not just seasonally) had reached 214, with sailing craft numbered at 371—the great majority of which were smacks. The *Beaconsfield* was still fishing, but she was very much what might be termed "yesterday's vessel".

10. Fifies & Dandies

The scene shown here was probably also shot from the end of the South Pier. Sailing drifters (both Lowestoft and Scottish craft) are seen making their way out to the fishing-grounds during the autumn herring season known as the *Home Fishing*. Beginning early on in October, and lasting a couple of months until early December, this was the great southern North Sea bonanza as the Downs stock of herring made its way southwards, in its millions—as it had done for centuries (if not millennia)— down to spawning-grounds on the Sandettie Bank, in the English Channel. This two-month fishing season had been the main foundation-block of Lowestoft's (and Great Yarmouth's) prosperity for the best part of six or seven hundred years when WRS took this photograph, and it hadn't been so very long before that Scottish fishermen had begun to sail south to take part in the annual reaping of the sea's harvest—a profitable way of extending their own summer fishery for herring. The first vessels to undertake the voyage, during the 1860s, were from the Firth of Forth area: ports such as Kirkaldy, Anstruther and the like, and their success drew in others from more northerly sectors of the Scottish East Coast. Peterhead, Fraserburgh, Banff and Buckie followed, then Wick—and, by the early years of the 20th century, even craft from the West Coast and the Hebrides became involved, as well as a noticeable presence from the Shetlands.

And it wasn't just the fishermen themselves who came. After a while, shore personnel who carried out the *Scotch cure* method of preservation arrived as well, by rail, in ever-increasing numbers, creating a livelihood not only for themselves but boosting the local Lowestoft economy also. Women (always known as "girls", regardless of their age) worked in gangs of three to process the fish: two to gut and size them and one to pack them into soft-wood barrels. The herrings were placed in layers inside, sardine-fashion, with each layer set

Fishing Boats. Lowestoft

at a right-angle to the previous one and with salt spread over it. Once full, supervising coopers headed the barrels up and left them for a number of days for the salt and fish-juices to mingle and form *blood-pickle*. During this process, the fish shrank and their level dropped inside the barrels. These were then opened up and fish of the same age of cure placed inside to restore them to full capacity. After being headed up again, they were ready for export abroad: mainly to Germany, Poland and Russia. Known originally as *white herrings* or *pickled herrings*, the particular method of cure had been started in southern Sweden with Baltic stock somewhere towards the end of the 13th century. The Dutch refined it further during the 16th and 17th, when fishing the North Sea, and the Scots further still during the 19th—placing their own name upon it. In Scotland itself, the barrels even had the distinctive outline of a crown burned into them, with the word "Scotland" beneath. It was known as the *Crown brand* and was the mark of assured quality. Depending on their size, there were between 900 and 1200 fish per barrel.

Traditionally, Lowestoft's own speciality was the *red herring*—a method of cure which had been practised since the late medieval period. The ungutted fish were dry-salted down on the ground, in heaps, on a prepared surface, and these heaps were then periodically *roused* (moved around) for two or three days with wooden shovels. The herrings were then washed, drained and allowed to dry, threaded onto *speets* (wooden rods made of coppiced hazel) through mouth and gill-case, hung in the fish-house and smoked over controlled slow-burning fires of ash or oak billets. A day's smoking was followed by a day's *resting*, to allow the fish to *sweat*—and the process continued for up to a month, depending on the *hardness* of the cure required. The fish were packed into casks and sent to destinations all over the country, as well as to near-European and

Mediterranean ports (particularly Leghorn—al. Livorno—in Italy). The processed fish was a product which could be cooked in a number of ways, and its long-lasting quality was an important consideration in an age without refrigeration. It remained an important element in Lowestoft's fish-curing industry right into the 20th century—its long and successful production not only the result of the curing process itself, but also of the physical condition of the East Anglian autumn herrings. These were ideal for *redding*, having a very low fat content of about 5-7% of body mass. The summer herrings of Scotland and the North-east of England could have as much as 20-25% and were much more perishable.

The vessel nearest the camera is a Scottish sailing drifter, known as a *fifie*, first developed on that part of the East Coast (Fifeshire) and ultimately reaching an overall length of around seventy feet. It had a vertical stem and stern, a long, straight keel, and a wide beam—all of this giving it great stability in the water, but lack of manoeuvrability also in confined spaces. Its two masts carried large, dipping *lugsails* and required skilful handling, but speeds of up to ten knots or so were possible in favourable conditions. Close examination of the men standing on the starboard side of the boat shows how low the sides of the craft were, relative to the level of the deck. There was no centre of gravity here worth speaking of! Ahead of the fifie is a local sailing drifter, operating mainsail, mizzen and foresail, but without *bonnets*, as the *Alert* had in the previous image. The port registration numbers on the sails of the two boats are difficult to read for the purposes of identification— impossible even, in the case of the fifie—but if the drifter is LT 303 (which seems a distinct possibility), then it is the *Chamois*. Both craft create a fine sight as they follow their fellow-vessels out to the fishing-grounds.

11. Smacks, Dandies & Fifies

Fishing Boats. Lowestoft —

A real mix of sailing vessels is seen here, with both of the two Lowestoft types of larger fishing craft shown, nearest the camera. On the left is a drifter (or *dandy*), named the *Pater* (LT 545), and on the right a trawler (or *smack*) called the *Forget-me-not* (LT 30). Both of them are towing their *little boats*, or dinghies, instead of having them secured inboard, amidships. Further out to sea, Scottish *fifies* are to be seen, discernible because of their dipping lugsails hoisted up on supporting *yards*. The nearest one is that detectable in the middle of the picture, out between the *Pater* and the *Forget-me-not*, while another is visible beyond the *Pater's* mizzen mast, which hasn't yet had its sail hoisted—thereby allowing the vessel to be seen. The texture of the sea's surface is well captured in this shot—the gentle ripple creating a sense of calm surrounding an occupation that was often dangerous in the extreme and had the highest death-rate of all types of work.

The sail-plans of the two nearest Lowestoft craft demonstrate the differences in the two modes of fishing practised. A *drifter* worked a whole series of cotton-fibre nets (each thirty or so yards long and about thirty feet deep), joined end to end, weighted down in the water by a long run of thick rope known as a *warp*, but also kept up near to the surface by periodic, inflated canvas floats known as *pellets* or *buffs*. Up to a mile or more in length of these nets was allowed to float in the upper reaches of the sea (having usually been cast by the crew, round about dusk) to enmesh the herring as they rose from the seabed, during the hours of darkness, to feed upon plankton. The vessel *drifted* along on the tide (hence its name), until the skipper decided that it was time to haul—and then the hard work began. The *steam capstan* wound the warp in, but the men had to haul the nets in over the side of the boat and shake the herrings from the meshes—a process that could take many hours in the event of large catches or adverse weather conditions. The writer has no specific information as to the number of nets carried by sailing drifters, but during the era of steam it was generally in the eighties or nineties (with some of the largest vessels of all exceeding this). Never an even number, however! Superstition required it to be an odd one. Thus, a vessel working eighty-three nets had a length of about one-and-a-half miles out ahead of it, as it drifted along on the tide, waiting for the herring to rise and strike the meshes.

A *trawler* dragged a large, tapering, cylindrical net (made of tough twine) along the seabed, to catch bottom-dwelling species such as plaice, soles, cod, whiting and rays of varying type. The top of the net's mouth was secured to a strong wooden *beam* (up to fifty feet in length) and usually made of two, equally-sized, hardwood, sapling tree-trunks *scarfed* together. Two large, iron, stirrup-shaped hoops (known as *trawl-heads*) were fixed to this at the ends and each of them had an *eye* in the bottom, into which a thick, heavy *ground-rope* was set, with enough slack in it to create an inward curve as the gear was dragged along the bottom, with the tide. Two *bridles* (one at either end of the beam) connected with a very heavy *warp* (thicker than a drifter's) and this was, in turn, secured to a stout *towing-post* amidships. The smack pulled this gear for the length of a tide usually six hours—unless a heavy catch was made before the time was up—and then the steam capstan did the donkey-work again, until the *cod-end* of the net was hoisted inboard and emptied—when gutting the catch begun.

And, so, to the different types of sail seen in the photograph and what they tell us about these two very different methods of fishing. It can be seen that the *Pater's* mainsail is *loose-footed*, without any kind of *boom* attached, and this was because the vessel simply drifted with the tide whilst fishing and had no need, then, of a boom, or when it was sailing to and from the fishing grounds. The *Forget-me-not*, on the other hand, had to drag a heavy beam-trawl along the seabed for hours at a time, with all the strain that this put on the mainsail particularly. Hence the boom fixed to it, to give extra strength and reinforcement. Apart from this difference in appearance, a smack could also be identified by the presence of its trawl-beam stowed along one side, with one of trawl-heads projecting beyond the stern. In Lowestoft's case, it was always the port side of the vessel, as can be seen here. Mizzen sails, on all fishing craft (even steam-boats, which retained them as part of their overall set-up), were less about providing motive power than keeping a boat stable and on course, both in varying weather conditions and as a means of assisting the work being carried out on board at a particular time.

Although the *Forget-me-not* is a Lowestoft-registered craft, she was not constructed in the port. Most locally built smacks tended to have the mizzen mast *rake* (lean) slightly forward from the vertical and, as can be seen, this vessel doesn't conform to that detail of design. Two other leading places in the construction of sailing trawlers were Rye and Brixham, both of which had craft working out of Lowestoft during the era of sail—and the *Forget-me-not* was, in fact, from the latter place. One of the writer's tape-recording respondents of the 1970s and 80s, who spent a number of years working on smacks as a young man, always said that vessels from the Sussex port were preferred to "Brickies", as they were of "stiffer" build and handled better in heavy weather conditions, in the North Sea, than boats which were designed for fishing the English Channel and the Western Approaches.

As well as their distinctive features, in terms of function and sail-plan, sailing drifters and trawlers also differed in size—which is suggested in the photograph, even though the *Pater* is further from the camera and slightly angled within the frame. Trawlers tended to be larger than drifters, the method of fishing carried out requiring a heavier build of hull and greater storage capacity down below in the fish-hold, where different species had to be sorted from each other and kept separate. As a generality, drifters tended to be somewhere between 30-40 *net tons* and trawlers 50-70, and the term "tons" had (and has) nothing to do with weight. It refers to a vessel's storage capacity, below decks, for cargo and equipment, with 100 cubic feet equalling 1 ton. *Gross tonnage* is the total under-deck cubic capacity, with all areas included regardless of their use.

41. The Herring Market (1)

Herring Market, Lowestoft

This view shows the area of the Lowestoft Fish Market devoted mainly (but not exclusively) to the sale of herrings and it was where the drifters landed their catches once they had returned to port. Samuel Morton Peto's improvements and extensions to the harbour works, carried out during the 1850s, had provided a single fish market along the original north pier on the seaward side of the bridge, but this proved too limited a facility before long. So successful were his modifications, as a whole—including the provision of railway links with Norwich, to begin with, and later with Ipswich-London—that the fishing industry quickly expanded as the result of a growing demand for its catches. Not only did the herring trade increase in both volume and capacity, but the introduction of trawling to the town (during the late 1840s to early 1850s) by vessels from Barking, on the north bank of the Thames, also created an increasing demand for demersal fish. These were species which lived on, or just above, the seabed and which had always been caught locally by either *hand-line* or *long-line* before trawling arrived.

During the early 1880s, as a means of accommodating a much larger number of fishing vessels, the Great Eastern Railway Company excavated and built a new wharf to the north of the outer harbour. This opened in October 1883 and was called the *Waveney Dock*. The photograph shows it with drifters at the quayside—there to land their catches—and with a long, roofed building running parallel to it, embellished with a decorative wooden pelmet. This was where the herring were taken for sale by auction and where some of them were salted down into barrels, on the spot, for further curative treatment elsewhere. The upper level of the landing-stage can be clearly seen on the left-hand side of the picture and there was a lower one, also—either one of them serving to function according to the level of the tide (the Trawl Dock also had this particular facility). Before the introduction of the *cran measure*, by Act of Parliament in 1908, as the official means of establishing the quantities of herring handled and sold, the fish had to be counted out by hand on board ship before being placed into baskets and put ashore. This long and laborious process had been in use for centuries and it was the custom to tally the fish in *warps*—a warp being four herrings, with two being held in each hand. Thirty warps added up to a *long hundred* (120 herrings, originally), but somewhere along the line, during the 19th century, the count had increased to thirty-three warps (132 fish)—the twelve extra ones being an introduction forced on fishermen, by the fish merchants, as a means of getting more for their money!

The cran measure itself (the word "cran" deriving from the Scottish Gaelic word *craun*, meaning a standard barrel of thirty-six gallons capacity) laid down a volume of thirty-seven and a half Imperial gallons as the official unit for recording and selling quantities of herring. Conveniently, this weighed out at 392 pounds of fish (regardless of size) which, when divided by four, produced ninety-eight pounds, or seven stones. Baskets of this capacity, holding seven stones of fish, were used to run the catches ashore from the drifters, using the steam capstan's pulley-wheel for motive power and a steam drifter's foremast gaff (or that on a sailing craft's mainmast) as a derrick, in tandem with a running-line secured to the basket's handles by a two-pronged metal grab known as a *cran-hook*. It was a much easier and quicker operation than counting the fish out by hand!

The men standing in the foreground may possibly be an assemblage of skippers, watching what's going on and having a conversation, leaving the handling and landing of the fish to their crews (this, after the *catch-samples* sent ashore for scrutiny by the merchants had been purchased at auction)—with the vessels' mates in charge of operations, as was customary. They're all wearing woollen *gansies* or calico *jumpers* (slops), with two of the latter—left and centre—new and untanned. Only the man on the right is jacketed. Not one of the group of eight is wearing sea-boots, now that the drifters have docked, and the headgear varies: three peaked nautical caps, two bowlers, and three soft, felt hats—one of which, worn by the man third from the right, looks for all the world like a precursor of the *trilby*, which wasn't known by that name until after George du Maurier had published his novel in the year 1893. The second vessel in from the camera (best detected as the one in front of two men on the right) appears to be a Scottish *fifie*, as a mast supporting a dipping lugsail is clearly visible.

19. The Herring Market (2)

Fish Market Lowestoft

This is another view of the area in the preceding photograph, with the previous image being closer to the dock. WRS stood further back for this shot, thereby revealing much more of the long, double-roofed building constituting the market-area itself. Once again (as in No. 41), a fifie is seen docked—this time nearest to the camera, with the foremast supporting a furled lugsail on its yard. Although *Herring Market* was a term generally employed for this part of the whole Fish Docks complex, the southern end of the trading-area's structure informs us that it was, in fact, the *Herring & Mackerel Market*. Also visible, on the right-hand section of the roof's gable is the second half of *Great Eastern Railway Company* and, although this feature cannot be seen, the cast-iron brackets of every post supporting the roof (one of which is clearly visible on the south-eastern corner) had the initials GER plainly displayed as part of their manufacture. High quality foundry-work was a distinguishing feature of the Victorian era, as was a capacity for creating industrial buildings of architectural merit—the one on show here being a good example. Even though it was effectively a large, open-sided shed, the elegance of the roof-line with its ridged coping and its excellent saw-toothed pelmet has created a building of real style. This probably wasn't of particular concern to the men who worked under its cover, or who landed fish there, but it certainly makes a statement to the observer of today regarding the age which produced it.

Mackerel had been part of the Lowestoft fishing effort from at least the 16th century, and probably earlier. The local season for catching them began off the Norfolk coast on grounds like the Cromer Knoll and

Winterton Ridge, and even on Smith's Knoll itself—best known as the North Sea's premier herring location. It ran from mid-May until the end of June, with the fish migrating southwards and ending up off Lowestoft itself. It never yielded large numbers (1,000-2,000 per trip being regarded as a satisfactory catch during the 18th century) and the mackerel were all sold fresh for local consumption because of their perishability and the time of year they were caught, probably reaching no further than Norwich. The drift-nets used to catch them were shorter than their herring counterparts, having a working length of twenty-one yards and a depth of about twenty feet, and they were made either of hempen twine or (later on) thick cotton—the mackerel's gill-covers being harder than those of herring, which meant that they could not be easily shaken from the meshes during hauling and had to be removed by hand, instead. This often resulted in the fishermen pricking themselves on the spiny dorsal fin—but these punctures bore no comparison with those inflicted by the so-called "horse mackerel", or Scad, which was no relative of the species but which often shoaled with it. These were hated by the fishermen, as they caused great discomfort and even infection, and because they had no commercial value beyond being sold for bait to craft engaged in line-fishing.

During the 1920s and 30s (very much the era of the steam drifter and drifter-trawler), the local mackerel voyage was still in operation—though on a much lesser scale than the autumn one for the herring. The catches landed were reckoned in *lasts* (12,000 fish) because the old, time-honoured *long hundred* measure was still being used to count them, without the *overtail/overtale* of twelve extra fish having been added to it. A total of 100 long hundreds added up to one last, and a one or one-and-a-half last catch was reckoned to be a good result, with a vessel of this time shooting in excess of 200 nets. And it wasn't only local waters that saw mackerel caught by Lowestoft vessels. As early as the 1860s (in a migration mirroring that from Fifeshire, down to East Anglia, to catch herring), drifters from the town were sailing to Cornwall each year, to take part in a fishing season lasting from late February through until May. Mounts Bay was one of the target-areas and so the boats based themselves at Newlyn and Penzance. It was a voyage which lasted over 100 years, finally coming to an end during the early 1950s—at which point, steam propulsion was rapidly being superseded by diesel power in fishing ports all over the country.

Thirty years or so into this Cornish fishing voyage, the Lowestoft men caused a major upset in the port of Newlyn, leading to the so-called *Newlyn Riots* of May 1896. The local Cornish fishermen did not put to sea on a Saturday evening or a Sunday—though this was not solely the result of a strict Sabbath observance encouraged by Methodist teaching (similar to that practised by many Scottish fishermen, under the influence of the Kirk's Presbyterian code). They also stayed in port so as to create a shortage of fish on the weekly Monday market, leading to catches being sold at premium prices on Tuesday. The East Anglian visitors sabotaged this commercial ploy by sailing on a Saturday evening and landing on Monday morning. Cornish discontent festered for a number of years, before things finally came to a head on the morning of Monday, 18 May. A company of some forty or more Newlyn fishermen, supported by hundreds of other townspeople, marched upon the harbour, boarded fifteen Lowestoft fishing craft and threw the catches overboard. Disorder continued the following day, when news of other returning "foreign" vessels (intending to land their catches at Penzance) led to large numbers of the local population to head there—only to be repelled by a strong police presence. The increased tension led to local magistrates sending for military assistance and the 2nd Battalion, Berkshire Regiment (which was stationed in Plymouth, at the time), duly arrived by rail to restore order. A Royal Navy destroyer, HMS *Ferret*, was also sent to provide a controlling presence and, eventually, an uneasy compromise was reached by the opposing sides. The Cornish fishermen agreed to the East Anglian vessels fishing on a Sunday (though predominantly from Lowestoft, there was a Great Yarmouth presence also), while the incomers conceded the Saturday evening practice of leaving port for the fishing-grounds. Neither side was completely happy with this arrangement, but the Cornish had the better of it, simply because it would have been extremely difficult to leave Newlyn or Penzance on a Sunday morning, get out to the fishing grounds, make a commercially worthwhile catch, and return early on Monday morning to sell it. Any vessel which was able to accomplish this would have been extremely lucky to hit a large shoal of mackerel as soon as the nets were in the sea.

The foreground of the photograph is dominated by large numbers of barrels for those herrings which were handled directly on the Market itself. They were packed—ungutted and dry-salted—into these casks, which were then sent elsewhere for other, specialist curative treatment, and they were known as *rough packs*. The barrels, made of spruce-wood for lightness and flexibility, are seen to be hooped with lengths of coppiced ash, split down the middle. At a later date, when managed woodlands were in decline, steel hoops succeeded them. At first glance, it may be thought that these containers were for the *Scotch cure* herrings, but the absence of any ends to seal them says otherwise. All the fish undergoing this particular process were carted off to various parts of the town where the *pickling plots* were located. A number of them were to be found situated off Whapload Road, conveniently close to the Fish Market, but other parts of the town had them as well—Norwich Road, for instance, in an area known as *The Brickfields*.

The other containers visible are the large wooden boxes with rope handles. These were for fish packed in ice, down on the market itself, finished with a layer of salt on top and headed up for export to Altona, in Germany. It became known as the *Klondyke trade*, its early years roughly coinciding with the Yukon gold-rush of 1896-99 and also producing wealth for the people who operated it. The enterprise lasted up until the outbreak of World War Two, but failed to re-establish itself afterwards. It was started by a Lowestoft fish merchant, Benjamin Bradbeer who, while visiting friends in Hamburg (for which Altona was the out-port), noticed the demand there for fresh herring. This was in 1887. His enquiries as to possible supplies of near-fresh Lowestoft fish were politely received, and so he sent some over on his return. The rest, as they say, is history!

So much to say about this image, and we finish once again with onlookers. Six of them are visible on the left-hand side of the picture, in two "threesomes". It is noticeable that the headgear is very similar to that in the photograph preceding this shot, and four untanned calico *jumpers* are to be seen this time instead of two. Skippers again, presumably, having a chat, while their crew members unload the catch after the sale-sample had had its auction price agreed. Three more white jumpers are visible further down the market area and drifter sails, on the upper right, reveal the presence of the boats themselves—stem on to the quay, as the fishermen themselves count out the catch and get it ashore.

13. Smacks Laid In

This collection of vessels are all sailing trawlers, as noted by WRS himself, with four of them able to be identified by their port registration numbers. Nearest the camera is the *General Gordon* (LT 348), named after the British military commander killed at Khartoum, in January 1885, during a Sudanese insurrection, who thereby became even more of a hero than he already was. Close by is the *Samuel & Emma* (LT 306) and, further removed, the *Walter & Emily* (LT 527) and the *Acme* (LT 651). The *Walter & Emily* is of particular interest, as she represents a piece of Lowestoft fishing history in miniature, belonging to a man called Walter Stock (and named either after himself and his wife or after two of his children), who is listed in *Huke's Directory of Lowestoft* (1892) as living not far from the harbour at No. 182 Denmark Road—*Thanet House*. The name of his dwelling gives a clue as to his origins, for he had sailed up from the coast of Kent (Ramsgate, specifically) at some point and settled in Lowestoft. He brought his household goods with him, on board, as well as his fishing-gear (though not in the vessel shown here)—part of that migration of trawl-fishermen from southern England, referred to earlier in the commentary relating to the first photograph shown in **Town and Surrounds**. The writer was fortunate to have made the acquaintance of his grandson, George, back during the mid-1970s, and to have tape-recorded his experiences of a life involved with fishing (along with those of many other local people) as part of a programme aimed at creating an archive of the Lowestoft industry, covering the years 1910-1960.

The smacks seen in the photograph are all laid in within the Trawl Dock area—except for the *General Gordon*, which is moored to the eastern section of the outer wall, near to the basin's entrance. The buildings seen in the background are ones which superseded earlier, Peto-era structures of the 1850s when the Waveney

Fishing Smacks

was constructed during the early 1880s to accommodate the increasing number of fishing vessels using the port. It was at that point that the former fish market, as it had been, became part of an area of activity devoted to trawling only—and even this soon needed revamping, in its own turn, to create mooring-space for the increasing numbers of craft involved. In 1891, the Trawl Basin itself was extended westwards, almost meeting up with London Road North. This photograph post-dates that reconstruction and it will not go unnoticed that the roof of the market building has the same wooden, saw-toothed pelmet as the herring-trading area of 1883. Nor will anyone looking at the image fail to see that the majority of the craft visible have lightly coloured sails (white, even), which shows that the shot was taken during the summer. At that time of year, many trawling smacks either used faded, older sails past their best or ones of less heavy canvas, since the weather conditions were generally kinder, and though treated with a waterproofing agent the latter type were not necessarily *tanned* with the same substance as that employed for winter sails. Only the *Samuel & Emma* is seen in her winter rig and these sails were generally treated with a mixture of red ochre, horse-fat and salt water—applied with *deck-swabs* as they were spread out on the ground, on the North Denes or any other convenient area within the town. This gave them a much darker, rufous hue, which was one of their most characteristic features and which is plain to see here.

Returning now to Walter Stock, to place him and his like within a wider Lowestoft context, he must have been living in the town for twenty years or so when this photograph was taken, as *White's Directory of Suffolk* (1872) places him and his family in Alma Street (no number given)—just off Bevan Street and adjoining Alma Road. He is described as "smack owner and fisherman", which means that he was almost certainly what would have been referred to at the time (and afterwards) as a "skipper-owner". He eventually worked his way up to owning four smacks—the *Volant* (LT 14), the *Cosmopolite* (LT 24) and the *Emily* (LT 249), in addition to the *Walter & Emily* itself—and it was this success which probably enabled him to move into a bigger house on Denmark Road. The area immediately to the north of this consisted of a network of densely packed back-streets and terraced housing, which resulted from the increase in population following on from the development of the harbour and coming of the railway, and Alma Street and Alma Road were but two of them. The western extremity of this complex had three very distinctive roads (referred to in the previous section) and promoted as the *Harbour Village* when the houses were built there during the early 1860s—to the designs of no less a personage than Peto's "in-house" architect J.L. Clemence. He even had one of the streets named after him (the middle one), to accompany those of Stevens and Selby, and Lucas Brothers built them—of course!

Alma Street and Alma Road had less impressive housing on them, but their names are significant nevertheless. The Battle of Alma was a British victory of the Crimean War, in September 1854—a conflict in which both Samuel Morton Peto and the Lucas Brothers played a notable role. The former built (at cost) seven miles of railway in just seven weeks (during February and March 1855) to convey munitions and supplies, from the harbour at Balaclava, up to an area of plateau which was being used as the base for the siege of Sebastopol— the ultimate fall of this stronghold being due in no small measure to its construction. A knighthood was duly conferred upon Peto (as head of Peto, Brassey & Betts) for this impressive feat of engineering and the railway carried not only ammunition and food for the troops, but also conveyed wounded soldiers in the other direction, thereby making it carrier of the first military hospital-train in the world. And this is where Lucas Brothers came in, for that company (allied so closely to Peto) made sectional wooden billets for those regiments engaged in the conflict at its joinery factory located on the southern side of the Inner Harbour at Lowestoft—as well as a similarly produced field-hospital for Florence Nightingale herself. An *Illustrated London News* of the time even shows some of the billets being loaded onto shipping moored alongside the company's quay—something which the publication obviously deemed worth making its readership aware of.

3. Tug & Smacks

A Great Eastern Railway harbour tug has four smacks in tow here, two by two, taking them out to sea beyond the harbour's pier heads—possibly (if the very calm waters are anything to go by) because the wind was not strong enough for them to make way unassisted. A fee was charged for this service and formed a means of creating revenue for the GER. The shot was taken from somewhere along the length of the South Pier, on its northern side, and seating for visitors and local people alike is plain to see in the bottom right-hand corner. The bowler-hatted gentleman close to WRS seems more interested in the rocks placed against the Pier as reinforcement to counter tidal action, rather than in the passage of the vessels themselves—but, there again, it could well have been just a momentary glance down which has been captured. On the far left-hand side of the picture—middle distance—the entry to, or exit from, the Waveney Dock area can just be seen. All four craft have both mainsail and mizzen set, and three of them are working topsails also—the one exception being the *Susie* (LT 28), the vessel nearest to the camera. Two rowing-boats are also discernible: one to starboard of the smack nearest the tug and another (harder to make out) over towards the wall of the Pier itself. What they were doing there is anyone's guess.

There was a tendency for Lowestoft men to prefer working on trawlers, rather than on drifters, as the fishing operation lasted all year round—compared with the seasonality of catching herrings and mackerel, which meant that the boats were often laid up when not in use and crew members laid off. Moreover, trawlermen were paid a weekly wage, with a little extra money sometimes deriving from the sale of under-sized fish and species which had little commercial value at market, such as gurnards and weevers (this small perquisite was known as *stocker bait*, or *stockie* for short). Herring fishermen, on the other hand, were paid on a share basis at the end of a fishing season, whereby if any profit had been made (after all expenses had been met) it was divided up among the crew on a basis of seniority and experience on board. In the event of a poor season, there would have been nothing to take up—the only positive for the men being that they had received their keep on board during the time that they were fishing. In the days before any kind of unemployment pay was introduced (1912), invoking Poor Law assistance and "going on the parish" was the only means of

Lowestoft Harbour

subsistence for the unemployed. And as is well known, even today, everybody hated the Workhouse and what it stood for!

This was why so many East Anglian farmworkers from inland communities within travelling distance of Lowestoft and Great Yarmouth (even if this meant walking—and it often did) would ship on board a herring drifter for the autumn home voyage. After the harvest was in, and the autumn ploughing carried out, many of them got laid off by the farmers they worked for until about February the following year. Increasing numbers of them, therefore, during the second half of the 19th century (as the fishing industry expanded), opted to go herring-catching and hoped to get a pay-off at the end of the voyage. They were all well used to hard manual work and most of them soon adjusted to life at sea. They were known as *joskins* (a word synonymous with "bumpkins"), *half-breed fishermen*, or even *half-and-halfers*, and they helped to fill a gap in the labour-force needed to crew sailing drifters—their muscle being especially useful to power hand-capstans when the nets were being hauled, in the days before steam capstans had arrived. The writer's maternal great-grandfather, Lyna Jones, was such a man—from the marshland village of Halvergate (some five miles or so inland from the port of Great Yarmouth). He drowned from off a herring drifter there, during the 1890s, while in his mid-twenties.

42. A Busy Trawl Market

Trawl Market. Lowestoft

This wasn't necessarily as crowded as it could get, but it does give some idea of the Trawl Market's level of activity when there was any quantity of fish to be landed. And the thought occurs, also, that the picture would present quite a challenge if it were a jigsaw puzzle! The vessel nearest the camera was the *Peerless* (LT 609) and a good deal of her working parts (to coin a phrase) is clearly visible. The mainmast with its boom and gaff are clear to see, as are the foresail and stay, and the bowsprit and its windlass—and the mizzen sail (on the photograph's extreme left) is at half-mast. There is a crew member, wearing a white *jumper*, aft-side of the furled foresail, but it is not possible to see what he is doing. The stern section of a smack in the bottom right-hand corner of the shot shows the after trawl-head of the trawl-beam itself, stowed port-side (as was the Lowestoft practice), overhanging the vessel's little boat. And the craft moored alongside has its *hoodway* (the entry to the cabin) clearly visible. Apart from that, there is little or nothing else that can be picked out to provide comment—except for the handle and parts of a sack-barrow's frame, with the arm of a crew member or fish-market worker holding it.

For the rest, the view is one of a veritable forest of masts, stays, ropes and halyards, showing that even after the Trawl Dock had undergone work to make it bigger there were still times when there wasn't enough room to swing a cod or whiting! Buildings are just about visible as a ghostly presence in the background, with the spire of St. John's Church among them—a place of worship designed by J.L. Clemence for the new seaside community, created by Samuel Morton Peto, and built 1853-4. One type of the stone from which it was constructed, Kentish Rag (the other being Caen) proved susceptible to the corrosive effect of the salty atmosphere and, though an impressive local landmark, it was demolished in 1978 (having been gutted by fire the previous year) and its parish merged with that of St. Peter's, Kirkley. Even before these final misfortunes had occurred, it had been made redundant and had stood sad and neglected—a target for periodic acts of vandalism.

47. Trawl Dock & Smacks

Trawl Market. Lowestoft

Another view of the Trawl Market, which appears to be less cluttered than the previous one, with the sailing trawlers all laid neatly broadside on to the quay and to each other. The vessel in the middle of the shot has the Ramsgate registration number R 32 and an initial attempt to identify it came up with the name *May Queen*, However, further investigation showed that this particular trawler wasn't built until 1897, so it is a predecessor which is seen here. The link between the Kentish port and Lowestoft has already been referred to in this section (in terms of human migration from there) and it is good, therefore, to see one of its boats at work in East Anglian waters—either because it belonged to an incomer who had settled in the town and hadn't been re-registered or because it had sailed up to Suffolk to carry out a summer fishing voyage. Ramsgate remained a place very much geared to sail, even after the introduction of steam power to fishing craft, and *Olsen's Fisherman's Nautical Almanack* for the year 1911 shows 174 fishing vessels of 15 net tons and above registered there—all of them sailing craft of one kind or another! An online site named *Ramsgate Registered Boats* is able to cast further light on its links with Lowestoft. It shows that H. Summers was the leading smack owner there during the late 19th century, and both *Huke's Directory of Lowestoft* (1892) and *Flood's Lowestoft Port Directory* (1903) show him to have been prominent in Lowestoft as well. The latter publication lists him as "Ramsgate" in its boatowner name-and-address column, so he had obviously opened up a trawling enterprise in Lowestoft while remaining resident in his home town. Three other men referred to in the Ramsgate data base (W. Caseley, P. Moxey and W. Painter) obviously moved their fishing operations to Lowestoft, as Walter Stock had done earlier—all of them listed as residents of the town in *Huke's Directory*.

Lying astern of the Ramsgate boat, and drawn up against a smack further in towards the quay, is a smaller, lower vessel whose hull is of lighter appearance (both in terms of build and of colour) than those of the smacks. This is one of the ice-wherries, which plied around the Trawl Market area supplying the boats with what was needed for their trips. Close scrutiny reveals that all the hatch-covers are in place, so perhaps it had not yet started to unload its cargo. It was sailing trawlers which used ice, rather than drifters, as they were out fishing for about five to seven days per trip, whereas drifters aimed at leaving harbour one day and returning the next with an overnight catch of herrings, fresh for the market. In the event of a meagre haul, they would salt those herrings down and try again the following evening, having to declare the first night's catch as *overdays* when they landed. These never fetched as much money as the fresh ones did, but would serve for certain kinds of curing—*kippering*, in particular.

Closest to the camera, on the extreme right-hand side of the frame, is part of a smack's bow section, the end of its retracted bowsprit clearly visible—which suggests that WRS was standing close to the southern edge of the Trawl Basin, to get the view he wanted. Furthest away from him is the Trawl Market building, with its characteristic pelmeted roof-line and, at the seaward end of it, a lookout tower known as *The Mount*. This provided a vantage-point for people to watch for vessels returning from sea—especially important during periods of stormy weather, but used also by local boys to earn small sums of pocket-money for themselves. They would climb the tower and, as soon as they had identified a returning smack, would run to the home of one (or more) of the crew members and inform the wife, or mother, that her husband/son was about to land. This small service was known as "running for a penny"—though sometimes, depending on circumstances, a ha'penny was the reward rather than a full penny itself or maybe something to eat, such as a sweet or two, or a biscuit.

There were two kinds of smacks operating out of Lowestoft, at this time: large ones of 50 net tons or more and smaller ones of 25-30 tons. The latter were known as *toshers* and they carried a crew of four (sometimes only three during the summer months), whereas their bigger counterparts carried five men all year round—or four adult males and a young lad not long out of school, who worked as cook and also learned the rudiments of fishing. Both vessels were more efficient at catching flatfish, which dwelt on the seabed itself, rather than the so-called *long fish* (whiting and cod). Hence, their mainstays tended to be plaice, dabs and soles, with the last-named of high value at market and given very careful treatment on board ship. Much smaller hauls of turbot, brill and lemon soles were also taken from time to time (depending on the grounds worked) and they, too, commanded a good price at market. Lower-value species such as roker (thornback ray), gurnards and weevers were further parts of the total catch, but never worth a great deal once landed. After the fish had come inboard and been released from the *cod-end* of the trawl, they were gutted, washed in tubs, drained in baskets and taken down to the fish-hold. This had boarded-off sections known as *pounds*, in which the different species were iced down and kept separate from each other—the ice being stored in a space of its own, insulated with tin or zinc. Once the vessel reached port, the more valuable fish (soles first!) were brought up from below and put into wooden boxes for sale on the Market (again, by auction)—the skipper and mate supervising the whole process to make sure that the best possible prices were secured. The lesser species were usually just heaped on the floor of the Market, to be sold.

HARBOUR VIEWS

12. Yacht Basin (with smack & gunboat moored)

Gunboat "Redwing" Lowestoft

This view was taken across the South Basin of the Outer Harbour, which had become known as the Yacht Basin by WRS's time because of the increasing use by yachts of the mooring facilities there. The Naval gunboat *Redwing* is seen tied up against its northern wall, and vessels belonging to the Royal Navy (notably those associated with Fisheries Protection duties) did indeed put into port from time to time on both courtesy and functional visits. The *Redwing* had been built in 1879 as HMS *Espion*, at the Pembroke Royal Dockyard, and was renamed a year later to replace a predecessor broken up in 1878. She was the first of the Banterer class, being of composite construction (iron keel, stem and stern-post, with a planked hull), steam-driven by a screw, and armed with two 6-inch and two 4-inch guns. It will be seen that her foremast is both square- and gaff-rigged, and that her main and mizzen are gaff-rigged only.

The sole smack keeping *Redwing* company is moored up closely to one of the *dolphins*—wooden structures placed at intervals around the basin, with a bollard on top on which to secure a rope. This feature can be clearly seen on all three of them, with the one on the right-hand side of the photograph having a secondary line running from the smack attached to it. The vessel's trawl-beam is stowed along the port-side rail, as was customary, and the net itself can be seen slung between the mainmast and the mizzen, hanging up to dry. A short break from fishing is obviously what is happening here, and the skipper is probably taking advantage of the generous amount of space available to carry out some on-board tasks. Two or three crew members are visible on deck, though there is no way of telling what they are doing. The contrast between the scene here and that portrayed in the last two images in the previous section could not be more marked.

The buildings in the background nearest the gunboat are part of a range of cattle sheds and stables servicing a cross-North Sea trade with Denmark in the importation of cattle, sheep, pigs and horses, begun by Samuel Morton Peto and operated by the North of Europe Steam Navigation Company. These stood near the bridge, beyond its approach and exit channel, on the Inner North Pier. Traffic in live animals began in 1850 and continued until 1864, when an epidemic of cattle disease and the war between Denmark and an Austro-Prussian alliance effectively brought it to an end. There had been financial trouble earlier, with major mismanagement causing the collapse of the North of Europe Company in 1859 and a take-over of operations by the Eastern Counties Railway Company (later to become the Great Eastern). Trade of sorts continued, though nothing like that which had flourished in its heyday. This trade perpetuated today in the names Denmark Road, Flensburgh Street and Tonning Street. The first one is self-explanatory, the other two the names of ports in former Denmark (now Germany), with Tönning also the name of a steam vessel involved in the trade. This, too, has its own place in the history of Lowestoft because its boiler once blew up while it was in port!

Just to the left of the livestock sheds, and to the rear of them, the thatched ice-house can be seen—a closer view of which was to be had in the **Town and Surrounds** section—and it is even just about possible to make out the harbour bridge. Or the position of it, at least, because it was located in the space between the gunboat and the smack. No sense at all is given here of the intervening stretch of water between the Inner North and the Inner South piers. For all practical purposes, at first glance, it isn't there. But it's not so much a case of the camera lying, as of the positioning of it by WRS as he stood somewhere on the western section of the South Pier (north side), looking across the Yacht Basin to focus on the two vessels moored there. There may have been others, out of shot, but it was this pair that he wished to capture and, in doing so, he produced a most evocative study. Two vessels of such contrasting appearance and function, moored within easy reach of each other.

4. Inner Harbour: Traders & Wherry

A fine view westwards, looking down the length of the Inner Harbour and taken from the southern side of the Bridge Channel, a little further along from where the concourse of people seen crossing the bridge (**Town and Surrounds** section) was shot. It shows a whole series of trading craft moored up along the northern quay, with the two nearest to the camera stern on to each other. The square-rig, which is visible on the foremast and main of each, with ketch-rig on the mizzen (the gaffs can be seen) identifies these craft as *barques*. These were real work-horses of the sea, at the time (if such a mixed metaphor is permitted), and carriers of cargo of all kinds, particularly timber from Scandinavia and the Baltic. The square-rigged two-master next to them is a *brig*, which has most likely brought coal into the port. Moving further down the harbour from these three craft, it becomes more and more difficult to recognise individual types of vessel, although the fourth one looks as if it might be a *billyboy*—a coasting trader of large capacity for its size, with origins on the Yorkshire coast.

The first three vessels described dwarf the *wherry*, which lies alongside the one nearest the bridge. Exactly what this local river-going craft is doing there can't really be ascertained, but it's almost certain to have offloaded something from its much larger neighbour, rather than to have put something aboard. Its skipper is visible standing on the hatch-covers, facing the camera, with his hands in his pockets, and its teenage boy can also be seen (both of them forming the wherry's crew) sitting on the same with his legs dangling—a pose which probably suggests that their work is done rather than not having been started. It certainly looks as if the mast has been used as a derrick, because it isn't locked into the vertical position in its *tabernacle*, but what the cargo may have been—who knows? Possibly not softwood timber into such a small craft,

Inner Harbour, Lowestoft

but maybe Russian hemp, Baltic grain, or even linseed for the oil-mill located further down the Harbour. Wherries carried enormous quantities of all kinds of merchandise on the waterways of south-east Norfolk and north-east Suffolk and were even able to make short sea voyages when, and if, required—as long as they kept reasonably close inshore and the weather was favourable. Thus, return-trips between Great Yarmouth and Lowestoft, and between Lowestoft and Southwold, are known to have taken place. And it is even possible that the vessel seen here, with its observable *sheer* (the hull's upward sweep to the bows) and its high hatch-framework, or *coamings*, could well have been built with that kind of passage in mind.

The building seen on the right-hand side of the photograph was the former engineering works of the North of Europe Steam Navigation Company, later becoming part of the Great Eastern Railway Company's Lowestoft operations. A little further along the quay, between the two barques, can be seen the three angled uprights of the *sheerlegs crane*. Known always, simply, as "the sheerlegs", the right-hand upright is most easily picked out because it is less obscured by ships' masts, yards and rigging than the other two. In the days of mass steam propulsion for the local fishing-fleet, it was much used to drop engines and boilers into newly-built vessels, but at the time this photograph was taken it probably served rather more for masting sailing craft and doing other heavy-lifting work. Even more of a visual "blast from the past" is the presence, in the bottom right-hand corner of the picture, of one of the masonry *knuckles* of the harbour's original sea-lock, with its timbered protection in place. As explained much earlier, in the **Introduction**, the lock failed quite early on in the harbour's history because of teredo worm attacking the timbers of its gates and making them inoperative. This then caused silting-up of the entrance to the Inner Harbour, which was one of the reasons why the overall enterprise became bankrupt.

For a great number of years, the overall supervision of Lowestoft Harbour, as a whole, had been the responsibility of the superintendent engineer, George Edwards. He was a man of great ability who, at some point in his long career, came up with the idea of fitting a metal flange onto the neck of an early diving-suit and bolting a helmet down onto it. He did not proceed with this revolutionary innovation, nor did he patent it, and thus missed out on the chance to make himself a considerable amount of money—to say nothing of a deserved acclaim in maritime circles. During dredging operations in the Inner Harbour, at some point, a large glacial erratic boulder (made of sandstone) came up in the grab and he kept it as a memento. When he died, it became his gravestone and can still be seen in the churchyard of St. Michael, Oulton. One side of it has been faced off and carries this inscription: **George Edwards C.E J.P. 1804-1893**. And that is all. Local tradition has it that it was his wish to have this sarsen stone as his grave-marker because, as an atheist, he had no wish to rise from Mother Earth on Judgement Day (like everyone else) and would therefore make sure that his own physical resurrection did not occur! That story would seem to be somewhat contradictory of a man who donated the land on which St. Mark's Church was built, during 1883-4, to serve the outlying part of Carlton Colville known as "Mutford Bridge", functioning as a chapel-of-ease to the parish church of St. Peter. The thought also occurs that if the artist, Stanley Spencer, had painted Oulton Churchyard, rather than the one at Cookham, in Berkshire, what would he have done with the mortal remains of George Edwards? Would the reconstituted body be seen rising from the place of burial or would it have been left where it had been interred?

18. The Dry Dock

Dry Dock, Lowestoft

An excellent close-up shot of the Inner Harbour's dry dock, located just down past the engineering works seen in the previous photograph. It was accessed both from the water and from Commercial Road, which ran parallel with the shoreline, and it is still in operation today, though all the timbering which can be seen here, on floor and walls, was replaced by concrete in 1928. The vessel nearest the camera is the smack *Pioneer* (LT 256) and there are six men on board her altogether—the hardest to pick out being the bowler-hatted figure just for'ad of the three located near the mainmast's shrouds. A fifth is seated under its boom, while the sixth and last is at the stern sitting beneath the mizzen's boom. A break from some maintenance work being carried out on deck, perhaps, or maybe even a request from WRS himself to "watch the birdie". One of the main uses of a dry dock, of course, is to carry out repairs or maintenance of that part of a vessel's hull which is below the water-line, but none of the three craft shown here give any specific clue as to what they may be in for. It could well have been something as straightforward as re-caulking the seams and re-sealing the planking with tar.

All of them are braced against the sides of the dock, and against each other, with supporting spars to maintain an upright position on the underlying timbers of the floor. Two men are walking around the right-hand side of the dock, perhaps to access the ladder pitched in its furthest corner, while a third (difficult to see) stands at its head, about to descend. Six others (there may even be a seventh hidden by the *Pioneer's* mizzen mast) stand along the left-hand side in varying poses of what may be termed relaxation—hands on hips or in pockets. As was the case with some of the onlookers in the two Herring Market scenes, in the previous section, four of the men seen here (one on either side of the dock and two on board the *Pioneer*) are wearing untanned *jumpers* and the usual mix of headgear is also a feature. The two on board—on close scrutiny—appear to be younger than the others with them on the vessel and those on the sides of the dock.

Among other details which take the eye are the *Pioneer's* little boat, and that of the craft in front of her, resting on the timbers of the floor, all of which are shaped to accommodate lower hull-sections and keels of varying sizes. The dock was originally built to service vessels belonging to the North European Steam Navigation Company, but was increasingly used over the years to assist maintenance work carried out on Lowestoft fishing-craft. The little boat of the smack in front of the *Pioneer* has the port registration number LT 621 visible on the stern, which makes it the *Norah Creina*—the name of an Irish folk song and one which Beethoven arranged (among others) and used to provide the main theme of his Seventh Symphony's last movement (1813). The third vessel is the *Electric* (LT 523), which presents a good stern-on view, showing its beam trawl stowed along the port side in typical Lowestoft fashion. Beyond the dock, and to the left of centre, the gable-end of the large building seen makes it absolutely clear that this is the premises of T. Saul & Son, Importers of Timber, etc., etc. *Huke's Directory of Lowestoft* (1892), in its business section, effectively gives what is probably much of the other information seen here in succinct and readable form. It declares that Saul, T. & Son, were "Timber, Slate and Cement Merchants and Sawmill Proprietors", based on Commercial Road.

All three smacks shown have their beam trawls stowed along the port side of the deck, with the after trawl-head of the *Electric* particularly noticeable. Another feature worth commenting on relates to the *Pioneer*. Between its main and mizzen masts, a stout wooden upright can be seen (slightly waisted in shape and with four projecting pieces—two of which are visible). This is the craft's *towing-post* or *dummy*, a timber which was set within the frame of the ship, below decks, and took the strain of the gear while trawling was in progress—a turn or two of the warp being taken around it to relieve the capstan (the name *dummy*, perhaps, deriving from any perceived similarity of shape with an infant's comforter). Details dating from the year 1896 and relating to this craft show that it had not yet converted to an Elliott & Garrood steam capstan, but was still using a hand-operated one.

Trawling as a means of fishing was first positively identified in public documentation in 1376, when a petition to the Crown sought to place limits on a new item of fishing-gear called the *wondyrchoun* (meaning, "a marvellous thing") which, it was claimed, was catching immature fish and destroying breeding-grounds and spawn in the Thames Estuary. It was said to resemble a *scrope-net*, something which was pushed or dragged along the seabed to catch oysters. An illustration shows it to have been an early beam trawl, with a beam probably no more than about 10 feet in length. The arguments about its destructive effect on the marine environment, it has to be said, have something of a modern ring about them, when modern beam trawls, with their steel beams and chain mats pulled along in front of the net to stir flatfish from the sand, come under fire for the damage they do to the seabed.

A century or more after the *wondyrchoun* was mentioned, a reference of 1491 shows such gear being banned in Orford Haven, further down the coast from Lowestoft—this time being called "an engine" (a common medieval term for any kind of mechanical device). The trawl just wasn't popular among most fishermen, who mainly caught demersal species with *hand-lines* or *long-lines*. And the opposition and arguments dragged on during the 16th and 17th centuries, and into the 18th, with periodic attempts to regulate use of the trawl and even define the size of its meshes. One particular declaration by the Lord Chief Justice, Edward Coke, in 1631, stipulated a net no longer than 24 feet on the beam and an overall length no longer than 48 feet. By the middle of the 18th century, the beam trawl had become pretty much accepted as standard fishing-gear and it is often this period which is cited in the matter of defining which English fishing station can be identified as "the cradle of trawling". Anyone from the South-west of England will make the claim for Brixham, while a citizen of the South-east will probably plump for Barking. The writer has to give the latter his vote, if only for the fact that it was the mouth of the River Thames where the beam trawl is first mentioned as being in use.

Trawling was a comparatively late arrival in Lowestoft, in terms of the town's overall fishing history, dating from c. 1850 when smacks from Barking began using the harbour and its facilities—something which they'd been doing in Great Yarmouth for perhaps approaching ten years or so. Up until then, Lowestoft's limited catches of demersal fish had largely been caught on hand-lines and long-lines, either by *herring luggers* working out of season or by smaller *longshore* craft working directly off the North Beach. Further removed in time, vessels from the town had sailed to Iceland each spring to take part in a hand-lining voyage for cod and ling, along with other vessels from the East Coast and also from Yorkshire—a venture which had begun in the earlier decades of the 15th century (possibly at Scarborough) and had ended by the middle of the 18th. North Sea trawling had been kick-started in the year 1837, when William Sudds, a Brixham man, discovered the Little Silver Pit fishing-ground on the Dogger Bank, together with its massive stocks of sole. Within a few years a bonanza was under way, with other grounds discovered and opened up, and Great Grimsby (to give the place its full name) had become a major centre of a trawling industry, especially after railway links inland were built. The Barking fishermen found themselves unable to muscle in on this operation to any great degree, using Grimsby itself, so they adopted Great Yarmouth and Lowestoft as substitute bases, with the latter increasingly used to work fishing-grounds between it and the Dutch coast: productive ones which had never been previously exploited.

9. Tug & Brigantine, Outward Bound

A fine study, here, of a *brigantine* being towed out of the harbour by a GER paddle-tug. The double funnels of the latter identify it as either the *Despatch* or the *Rainbow* and with the outpouring of smoke from these adding greatly to the photograph's scenic effect—even if doing little for the control of noxious chemical emissions! Three staysails are set between the brigantine's mainmast and foremast, a loosely furled headsail is in position at the end of the bowsprit, and there appears to be a single crew-member (just discernible) standing in front of the main, looking out towards the camera and its operator. The vessel is just about to clear the Inner North Pier (the harbour's original one before later extensions and improvements were made) and the Trawl Market can be seen beyond it, with smacks moored up in the dock evident by their masts showing. The Mount lookout-tower is also a prominent feature here, the interlacing of its timbers noticeable against the backdrop of the sky—a feature which was both structural and functional and therefore pleasing to the eye. Beyond the entry to both market areas (Trawl and Herring-Mackerel), in the middle distance, some kind of harbour works are in progress, with a steam-crane in use, possibly carrying out lifting work of some kind or even dredging operations.

The brigantine seen here might well have been on a return journey to the North-east of England, having brought a cargo of coal to Lowestoft from the mines of Yorkshire, Durham or Northumberland. This carriage had been going on since, at least, early Tudor times and the Newcastle Chamberlains' accounts for the first decade of the 16th century make reference to it. At that time, the coal was not solely for Lowestoft, and probably mainly intended for London, but it was offloaded in the town's inshore reaches and brought to land by ferry-boat—the construction of the harbour being over three centuries away. Long before it had its harbour, the town was an important stopping-off place for coastal trading-vessels, to take on supplies of fresh water and food items, as well as marine stores if needed, and it also served to give safe anchorage to any craft which found itself threatened by the weather. The offloading of coal locally was mainly for domestic use in the houses of the wealthier members of the local population and it is interesting to note that, as early as 6 May 1580, a chimneysweep (Wyllyam Garret, by name) is recorded in his wife's burial-entry in the registers of St. Margaret's parish church. By the early 18th century, "a place to lay coals" is an expression increasingly found in connection with Lowestoft houses, even among the less affluent levels of society.

Lowestoft

21. Steam Yacht *Gabrielle*

"Gabrielle" Lowestoft Harbour.

An interesting, close-up study, here, of a "high-end" luxury steam yacht, which is comparable with the photograph featured in Volume I of WRS's work (p. 46), which was taken of the Duke of Hamilton's vessel, *Thistle*, in Ipswich Docks. The *Gabrielle* matches that particular vessel in having three masts, as well as an engine, but no useful further comparisons can really be made because of this shot not showing the whole length of the craft. It looks as if WRS was standing at the end of the eastern wall of the Yacht Basin to take this picture, with his subject angled in front of him. The Inner South Pier (forming the north wall of the Yacht Basin) is clearly visible in the middle distance, with the bridge-approach situated beyond it (not seen), and the old North of Europe Steam Navigation Company's cattle-sheds and stabling-areas are plain to see, standing along the Inner North Pier. The Trawl Market's presence beyond them is marked by The Mount lookout tower. Slightly closer at hand than that particular feature, a pair of funnels seen through the port-side shrouds of the *Gabrielle* indicates that a GER tug is moored in the Outer Harbour's central channel.

There are two men to be seen on the steam yacht's starboard side, amidships, carrying out tasks of some kind, and a third is visible standing between the engine-room's ventilators apparently doing work on the left-hand one. All of them may have been members of the crew, but it is equally possible that they were employees of a local company which specialised in marine maintenance and repair. The vessel's port-side lifeboat can be seen slung from its *davit*, beyond the funnel and ventilators, but the starboard one is missing. A sailing craft occupies the foreground, but there seems to be a smaller boat between it and the steam yacht, in which the man clad in white is standing as he performs some task near the entry *gang* cut through the yacht's gunwale. Perhaps this was the starboard lifeboat. Two further vessels appear to be moored off to the port side of her, the closer of them with a lifeboat secured to its davit. The whole scene is one in which the viewer is left feeling that if WRS had chosen (or been able) to stand a little further back, more sense could be made of what was taking place. As things stand, the shot is certainly one of interest, but with questions remaining which have to be left unanswered. The same is true of the *Gabrielle* herself, in terms of provenance. Attempts to trace her origins have been made and proved unsuccessful, but her presence here in Lowestoft shows that someone of considerable wealth had put into port for whatever the reasons.

39. Yacht Basin Scene

Yacht Basin, Lowestoft

It is worth making comparisons between the scene shown here and that on view in the first photograph featuring in this section. The latter shows the Yacht Basin with only two vessels moored in what could be seen of it, whereas there are nine substantially-sized yachts here occupying the central part of the dock and at least four smaller sailing craft also in sight—to say nothing of various dinghies and rowing-boats. A line of four *dolphins* can be seen running down the length of the dock, left of centre, with mooring-lines clearly attached to the one nearest the camera, and a number of gentlemen seemingly clad in yachting attire (caps, jackets or blazers, and at least one pair of white trousers) can be seen on the central pair of the four vessels in the foreground. Originally known as the South Basin, this part of the Outer Harbour had been aimed at mixed use by different kinds of craft, but it became increasingly associated with yachts as time went on—something which reflects the growing popularity of sailing as a leisure occupation among the well-to-do classes of mid-late Victorian society.

The Norfolk & Suffolk Yacht Club was formed on 9 April 1859, its stated intention being to promote yacht-racing on local rivers and broads. The original headquarters was in Norwich, but in 1884 it was decided to build a small clubhouse at Lowestoft on land leased from the Great Eastern Railway Company. This was on the west side of the basin—still, the location of the club's present-day HQ. In 1898, the society added "Royal" to its name, by Crown warrant—an act confirmed later by Edward VII, when he had succeeded his mother, Victoria, as monarch. And so the Royal Norfolk & Suffolk Yacht Club had well and truly arrived on the local social scene—though its RN&SYC initials did become parodied at some stage with reference made by local people to either the "Royal Nobs and Snobs" or the "Royal Nobs and Sods", depending on who you talked to. The new clubhouse opened in 1886, but such was the popularity of the club itself that its increasing membership soon required a bigger premises. G. J. Skipper, of Norwich, won the competition to design it and the building was erected during 1902-3. It is one of only three structures in the town to carry a Grade II* listing—the other two being the Lighthouse and No. 36 High Street (St. Margaret's Parish Church is Grade I)—and it is an excellent example of the Arts and Crafts style of architecture. Skipper was a fine exponent of this, but he was influenced by (arguably) the best of all English architects of that period, C.F.A. Voysey, whose hand is to be seen all over the Yacht Club's exterior and in some interior features as well.

The background of this photograph gives a real sense of scale—at least, as far as the buildings of the Peto-era are concerned—for these are a dominant feature, even though some distance away from the camera. The original N&SYC clubhouse is plainly visible in the middle ground, its light decoration and single-storey construction contrasting strongly and effectively with its surrounds and making an aesthetic statement of its own. Behind it, on its right-hand side (to the reader), is the *Harbour Hotel*, while to the left stands the first of the grand Esplanade villas which were responsible *in toto* for the dwellings that made up Marine Parade being described as "excellent second-rate houses". The second one along from this is also visible and, between the pair of them and further removed, can be seen the tower of J.L. Clemence's St. John's Church— two of its four clocks prominent on the spire. No less impressive are the buildings of the southern part of Pier Terrace, (situated beyond the *Harbour Hotel*), a row of shops with living accommodation above, on the turn into Belvedere Road. The other part of this complex lay to the north of the Bridge Channel, up to the corner of Commercial Road, and *Huke's Directory of Lowestoft* (1892) notes that numbered among all of these retail premises were a chemist, a boot and shoe manufacturer, a photographer, a confectioner, and a wine & spirit merchant. Over to the right of the picture, and further removed still, the mast and yards of trading vessels in the Inner Harbour can be seen, while on the extreme right stands the engineering works of the former North of Europe Steam Navigation Company. The number of people visible in the shot (especially around the entry-area to the South Pier) suggests that there may have been something special going on, such as the annual Regatta in late August. Or perhaps it was just another busy holiday weekend.

40. Yacht Basin & Bridge Approach

A superb shot of the north-eastern sector of the Yacht Basin, clearly showing the sea-approach to the harbour bridge with the former cattle sheds and stabling-range of the North of Europe Steam Navigation Company standing along the Inner North Pier. The Trawl Market area is defined by its distinctive lookout, and the thatched roof of the ice-house can also be seen beyond the masts of the *barque* moored up alongside the pier. Visually speaking, two of the most eye-catching features in this view are the decorative woodwork of the range of buildings on its right-hand side and the lovely continuous run of slatted timber forming the seating on the Yacht Basin's eastern pier. Its gently curving profile and elegant semi-circular sweep at the northern end is sheer perfection and speaks well of a process which could make something as basic as somewhere to sit into a statement of elegance. Its clean lines and smart appearance contrast noticeably with the stilted timbering of the pier which it surmounts –this being weathered by permanent contact with tidal water, day in and day out.

On the far left of the photograph, people appear to be queuing for a pleasure-trip out to sea on the volunteer lifeboat *Carolina Hamilton*, as it prepares to tie up and discharge its previous load of passengers. Presented to the town by Lord Claud Hamilton (Chairman of the Great Eastern Railway Company) and named after

Lowestoft

his wife, it carried out rather more of this kind work than it did rescuing distressed mariners, though its usual place of operation was just inside the harbour's South Pierhead. Next to it, the harbour paddle-tug *Imperial* can be seen moored, its boiler under steam if the smoke gently issuing from its funnel is anything to go by. And, last of all, to occupy this side of the basin, at its entrance, is the paddle-tug *Express* (belonging to the Great Yarmouth Steam Tug Company)—seemingly about to leave port with a full complement of passengers on board, to make a short trip up or down the coast somewhere, before returning to Lowestoft. A number of the Yarmouth tugs did this kind of work during the summer months—the neighbouring port not being as busy, then, as at other times of the year—especially during the autumn, when the herring season was in full swing. A group of five or six ladies, standing at the end of the eastern pier, appear to be taking in the scene, while on the left-hand side of the picture a couple of men (dressed in less elegant apparel) seem far more interested in a single, small boat being rowed across the basin. Also under propulsion by oar (four of them) is the *gig* making its way out of the basin—the men doing the work being the four local coastguards, if their caps and blue-jean collars (al. *tar-flaps*) are anything to go by. They lived in a row of cottages set back from Battery Green Road, at the eastern end of The Marina. The buildings are still there—except that, after changes to the local highways system, they are now designated as being part of Gordon Road.

As a final word on this scene, of what may be termed water-orientated enjoyment, there is also at least one reminder that a busy town lay situated close by, to the immediate north of the harbour, with retail shops of many different kinds. Just to the right of the top of the outermost flag-staff, on the eastern pier of the Yacht Basin, the word TUTTLE can be seen on a gable-end of one of the buildings visible in the background, advertising the presence of the *Bon Marche* drapery and general furnishing store. The proprietor, Henry Tuttle, and his son Ebenezer were well-known figures in the town—the latter serving as mayor in 1904-5 and 1906-7.

8. Regatta Day: Yacht Basin

Regatta Day Lowestoft

No guesses here as to what's going on! The assembled craft, with bunting prominently displayed, show that this is Regatta Day—Lowestoft's brief period of maritime celebration, when the working world of herring-drifter, smack, yawl and longshore boat combined with the affluent, leisured world of sailing for pleasure and competitive challenge. The yachts lined up along the *dolphins* represent a world far beyond that of the local fishermen in terms of affluence (but not necessarily among, at least, a number of the more important vessel-owners) and the meeting of the two represented, if not the full extremes of late Victorian society, then at least a substantial cross-section of it. And then, of course, there were the visitors who came from places beyond Lowestoft, to view the summer spectacle and feel themselves part of it.

In all likelihood, the event had begun much earlier on in the 19th century, because William White's *History, Gazetteer & Directory of Suffolk* (1844) describes two notable "water frolics" of the time: one taking place on Oulton's broad in July and another on Lake Lothing in August. Presumably, the latter's use as the town's Inner Harbour had not sufficiently developed at the time to prevent water-borne leisure activities from taking place and being enjoyed. However, following on from Samuel Morton Peto's innovations of the 1850s, and the consequent increase in both fishing and mercantile trade, things probably changed and it was likely that any sporting and competitive aspects of the "frolic" then moved eastwards to the sea. The formation of the Norfolk and Suffolk Yacht Club in 1859 (later to become "Royal") may also have been another factor in a new venue for the event being adopted and it wasn't long before it became a major East Coast attraction.

There appears to have been no permanently fixed date for it to take place. White's *Directory* simply says August. Nine years later, on an engraving of the "Regatta" (and that is the word used) taken from the Esplanade, a date of 23 July 1853 is given. A Ward Lock Guide Book of 1937, *Lowestoft and District*, says "the end of August" (pp. 2-3) and this ties in with what some of the writer's tape-recording respondents said while recounting their herring-catching experiences. They all agreed that the summer voyage to Shetland, ending with a few nights fishing off North Shields and Scarborough, on the way home, needed to be finished in time to get back to Lowestoft for the Regatta—at the end of August. Once the event had passed, then it was time to get the drifters ready for the major season of the year: the autumn Home Fishing.

Returning now, to the photograph, apart from the yachts themselves, the other vessel worthy of close attention is the one nearest the camera—a fine steam-launch of the period, with beautifully upswept bows. Its funnel, emitting smoke, can be seen projecting through the protective awning which guards against both rain and shine, and there is someone sitting beneath it aft-side—perhaps the owner. Its presence represents another aspect of water-related leisure activity and enjoyment for the wealthier members of late Victorian society and it is, in its way, an even more iconic craft of those times than the yachts which are present. In the middle of it all (at least as far as this scene is concerned), and just off to the left of the mast which occupies the central point, the rounded cover of a harbour tug's paddle-wheel can just about be seen—while, on the left-hand side particularly, the tanned sails of trawling smacks create a faded back-drop to give another reminder of the everyday, working world.

43. Regatta Day: South Pier

Lowestoft Pier

Although not entitled so by WRS himself, this looks likely to have been another Regatta Day scene—one captured looking along the length of the South Pier out to sea. Most Victorian piers were built out from the shoreline purely as leisure facilities, but the one here at Lowestoft was of dual function. Along with its northern, differently-shaped counterpart, it was constructed not only to provide extra quay-space within the water impounded, but to provide sufficient capacity for the flushing action of the sea's ebbing tidal-flow to keep the Harbour mouth and bridge channel free of silt. Once the original lock-gates had begun to fail during the late 1830s and had not been replaced, another solution had to be found to counter the build-up of sediments. Peto's extension of the harbour-works provided this, but with the intention also of making the southern pier a public amenity to accompany his development of the shoreline as a model seaside resort of the time. The plan worked well and the South Pier became a key visitor attraction among the many other delights Lowestoft had to offer. A set of commemorative lithographs (in both coloured and monochrome form) were produced by the artist, H.C. Trery, in 1852 and dedicated to Peto himself. Among the subjects chosen for illustration was the South Pier.

A mixture of vessels is on show, to draw the attention of the watching crowds strung out along the length of the pier and gathered at its end—but exactly what all of these craft are doing together here is not clear. The most noticeable vessel, in terms of its size, is the herring drifter (or *dandy*) *Qui Vive,* identifiable by its port registration number LT 147 and sporting almost a whole complement of sails, with only a jib missing. Astern of it is a local *shrimper*, with mainsail and topsail set—very much the craft of Lowestoft's *longshore* fishermen, many of whom lived on The Grit ("Beach Village", to more poetic souls) and made a bare living from the waves. Yes, they trawled inshore for shrimps during the summer months (and visitors and local people alike loved them), but they also changed over to a larger-meshed trawl and went for soles—usually their most valuable catch if they could get ones of the right size. And that was only part of it. October and November saw drift-netting for herring, close in, followed by sprats during the winter itself, a period also spent long-lining for cod and other demersal species, as well as trawling for whatever species offered themselves. Longshoring was, in every way, an all-year-round occcupation, with wives and children part of a team effort to maintain and service fishing-gear and help also to keep the boats in good repair.

Owing either to over-exposure in the taking of it or to aberrations in the developing of this particular photograph, much of the seaward part of the shot is very pale. This makes it difficult to see everything clearly and certain vessels have little or no definition at all. The one just beyond the *Qui Vive*, and to port of it, does not present enough of itself, leaving only the rowing boat with three figures on board (nearest the camera) and the two *yawls* beyond it able to draw comment. The former may be part of whatever is going on or its occupants may just have rowed out there to get a better view. And the yawls might just be racing each other in a rowing contest, because both are being propelled by oar and because such matches did take place at local regattas—though usually on a much larger scale. It is even possible that what we have here is a head-to-head between the two Lowestoft beach companies, the Old Company and the Young. Both had their headquarters in large wooden sheds (or *shods*) down on The Grit and their members involved themselves in salvage-work and life-saving activities when not fishing along the shoreline. The yawls (with their smaller cousins, the *gigs*) being essential craft in carrying out such endeavours.

Reference was made in the preceding set of comments to a Regatta Day date of 23 July 1853. The drawing made that day, to produce the engraving, shows a yawl race taking place, with onlookers standing on the South Pier, on the Beach and on the Esplanade. The number of vessels taking part is something like ten to twelve (it is hard to be absolutely sure), all of them under sail, which means that some of the beach companies from up and down the coast were probably participating: Pakefield, Kessingland and Southwold to the south and Gorleston, Great Yarmouth and Caister to the north. The two yawls seen here do appear to be the focus of attention, from the way that the onlookers seem to be studying them. One little boy is seen in the foreground, kneeling on the seating and taking everything in, his sailor-suit clothing and headgear being so typical of the time and appropriate for this setting. Is the one who has just walked past him his brother (a twin, even), holding onto the hand of a parent hidden by the nearest set of flags? Who knows? Most of the flags do seem to be responding to the breeze, though not to the extent of being fully extended. One set, just to the left of centre (the pole, or staff, almost invisible) has the middle one twisted in such a way as to resemble the world's biggest seagull. Imagine that diving down onto your fish-and-chips! Though, there again, such an avian creation would still be nowhere near the size of that monstrous bird of Sinbad the Sailor's second voyage, the legendary Roc of old Arabia.

51. The Pierheads

Lowestoft

Again, a somewhat faded image (especially on the left-hand side), showing the twin Pierheads of the Harbour entrance with their elegant and distinctive lighthouses—the latter built to show the way into port during the hours of darkness. Again, as in other views already presented, what we have here is something functional built with an elegance of design which transcends the ordinary and everyday and lifts both the eye and the spirit with its quality. The same may also be said of the wooden rail surmounting both pierheads' timbering, as it rises from the water. The cross-pieces inserted between the uprights were put there as a safety measure, and verticals or horizontals would have sufficed. But how much more pleasing on the eye to have these diagonals installed. It's not so much a case of the devil being in the detail, as the delight to be found there! The southern Pierhead is thronged with people, whereas the one on the north has hardly anyone on it. This was largely due to a problem of accessibility. The former was at the end of a straight, relatively short stroll along something built with promenading partly in mind. The latter meant trekking past the Trawl Dock, along behind the back of the Herring Market, before continuing on down to the end of the North Extension. A much more circuitous route and one likely to leave your shoes in a mess!

The main thing to take the eye in this shot is another Yarmouth paddle-tug (no name discernible, this time) coming in to port with a load of day-trippers on board, passing an outgoing yacht as it enters. The sail of the latter is almost impossible to discern, but the vessel's boom shows that it is there and three members of her crew are also plain to see. Someone is standing close to WRS, rolled newspaper in hand, and just beyond this a set of steps (or, at least, part of it) can be seen ascending from the water to a gateway in the Pierhead's rail. This was to provide access to the *Carolina Hamilton*, the volunteer lifeboat which featured three photographs previously, for this was its usual mooring-place—sometimes to be seen with the vessel *in situ* in later, Edwardian-period postcards. Although the gift of this craft to the town by the Chairman of the GER in 1883 was a generous one, it was in some ways misguided. Life-saving operations in the town were carried out from the North Beach, by members of the two beach companies using their yawls and manning the two RNLI vessels (the *Samuel Plimsoll* and the *Stock Exchange*) which were kept on station there. This made a third lifeboat superfluous, and the place where it ended up being moored was not at all conveniently located for anyone to man it in an emergency. And not just in terms of being easy to reach. Most of the people living in the houses forming Peto's model resort were hardly suited to crewing lifeboats.

57. A Lifeboat Quartet

Aug. 22nd 1892

   This photograph is one of only four in the whole collection to have the date recorded (the other three featuring in the following section) and all of them show considerable fading. Owing to this, and relating specifically to this picture's background, it is difficult to positively identify the location—but it looks as if it might be the Waveney Dock. It that is the case, then the vessel furthest from the camera and showing the numbers 98 might possibly be the herring drifter *Duke of Connaught* (LT 98). From what can be seen of it, it doesn't look like a smack and there's no trawl-beam present, stowed along the port-side rail of the vessel. WRS has given no information regarding this shot, but has simply dated it as shown above. And this date may possibly give a clue as to what was happening in the town at that time because, with 22nd August being a Monday, it could mean that the annual Regatta was to be staged during the approaching weekend. The local Home Fishing period was still about six weeks away and there would have been spare capacity in the Waveney Dock for visiting vessels to moor—such as the four lifeboats seen here.

However, there is a problem with the dating given by WRS, because it is known that national lifeboat trials took place at Lowestoft during February 1892, starting on the 11th (a Friday) and lasting a week. The *Henry Richardson*, from New Brighton on Merseyside, was present, as was a new Watson-type craft straight from the maker's yard in Glasgow (seen next to her) and an RNLI self-righting craft sent up from London (third vessel along). The fourth boat, of which very little can be seen, was probably Lowestoft's second lifeboat, *Stock Exchange* (the *Samuel Plimsoll* being No. 1), which also took part in the trials. It seems likely, then, that the trials held are what led to this photograph being taken, but no explanation can be given for WRS's dating of it. Suffice it to say that the Waveney (al. Herring) Dock would have been as relatively free of drifters during February as it would have been in August, so there would have been plenty of space for other craft to make use of it. Of the four lifeboats present, three were propelled by sail and oar ("sailing and pulling" craft, as they were known), but the *Henry Richardson* was oars only and its rowlocks can be seen on either gunwale.

A conversation can be seen taking place between a crew member of the *Stock Exchange* (seen standing at the stern, with someone sitting below him) and the two men standing on the drifter (they probably knew each other)—and, while this is going on, another man (wearing a typical *sou-wester* of the time, with extended neck protection) is bending to some task or other. From what little can be seen of it, amidships, the *Stock Exchange* appears to be much more like the *Henry Richardson* than the two interposing boats, with metal uprights placed along the gunwales and a rope restrainer running through the eyes. The two larger lifeboats both have what appear to be plaques of some kind mounted on the bow, but unfortunately even the more visible of these cannot be read. If the one to be seen on the restored Southwold lifeboat *Alfred Corry* (housed in the town's museum dedicated to the craft) is anything to go by, they will say NATIONAL LIFE BOAT INSTITUTION, with the first and last words placed above and below the middle two.

Two of the local shrimpers lie astern of the biggest lifeboat, their trawl-nets drawn up the masts to dry, while a larger vessel on the extreme right of the picture is being pushed clear of the other vessels by one of its crew, using a *quant*. In a sense, what we have in this picture is a meeting of two worlds: that of everyday work related to fishing and that of rescue at sea, whereby people of all kinds, in many different types of craft, were saved from drowning when their vessels found themselves in the most desperate of situations. Holding national RNLI trials at Lowestoft was entirely appropriate, as the town had the distinction of having been a lifeboat station since the year 1801 and also of having had the country's first craft propelled by both sails and oars. This was the famous *Frances Ann*, which came into use in 1807, remained in operation until 1850, and saved over 300 lives. There is a notable picture of this vessel being launched off the North Beach into stormy seas, in the year 1821, by the Great Yarmouth marine artist John Cantiloe Joy—though some attributions state that it was in collaboration with his older brother, William.

1. Dredging Operation

The caption used by WRS for this particular photograph does not specify which of the Harbour's piers is being referred to and, once again, the faded nature of much of the print makes precise identification of its location difficult. There is, of course, no problem in working out what is happening here. On the left of the picture, a GER steam-crane is being used to carry out dredging work, its grab being clear to see, as well as the operator standing between the winch and the boiler. A line of railway wagons are drawn up behind it, with the two to the left (only one of which can be fully seen) containing spoil. At least one more must be hidden by the machinery, while the two to its right appear to be empty. All of them are standing on rails which must have been laid down, as a temporary measure, for the work to take place—the only permanent track in the Outer Harbour area being that which connected the Railway Station with the Fish Market, running alongside the Trawl Dock before turning northwards to service the Waveney Dock and its landing-area.

The disturbance on the surface of the water, with noticeable wavelets present, shows that this is the approach to the bridge being dredged. The steam-crane and wagons are therefore standing on the Inner North Pier (the

From Pier. Lowestoft

dump-end visible, at the entrance to the Trawl Dock), with WRS and his camera placed on its Inner South counterpart. To the right of centre, the GER steam suction-dredger *Pioneer* has mooring-lines running to either pier as it carries out its own work in the middle of the channel. Iron-built in 1886 at Stockton-on-Tees and driven by a single screw, it remained in use at Lowestoft until, at least, the 1950s, having been converted to diesel power at some stage. It was broken up in 1963 and is a dominating presence in the picture, with its broad hull, its blunt, head-on appearance, and the strong, uncompromising line of its funnel. One of the crew can be seen standing to starboard, between the side of the vessel and the engine-room ventilator, and its lifeboat is moored alongside ready to be used when needed. At some point, after this shot was taken, it was joined by a sister-ship, the *Progress,* and a photograph (held in the Suffolk Record Office collection) shows both vessels coming into port—though no specific date is given.

It might be thought that, given the reach of the crane, little would have been achieved by clearing along the side of a pier, but this was where a build-up of sediment would also have occurred, as well as in the middle of the channel. Dredging the Harbour entrance, the individual basins and, of course, the Inner Harbour also was work which had to be regularly carried out for the port to function effectively. It wasn't the sort of activity, in a holiday resort, which would have appealed to a professional photographer looking to capture appropriate scenes (especially after the turn of the 20th century, when postcards became increasingly popular), but it obviously took the eye of an amateur one. We should all be thankful that it did, as it gives us the opportunity to see something essential to the smooth operation of the harbour, which would otherwise have gone unrecorded.

RESORT ACTIVITY

14. South Beach & Pier, Whit Monday

Lowestoft Beach   Whit Monday.

No date is given for this view, to say which year the photograph was taken, but it appears to be fine weather and the bank holiday crowds are out in force. The Pier itself, seen as just one long, almost-unbroken run down to its terminating lighthouse, looks as if something is missing—and there is! The single-storey Reading Room (a rectangular building of quality, with low-profile roof, overhanging soffits, decorative cornices and ornate doorways east and west) had burned down in 1885 and was later replaced by a large and imposing Pavilion, which opened in 1891. The Reading Room obviously served more purposes that its titular one, because photographs of it show that the edges of the roof formed a viewing balcony with an elegant cast-iron rail, and summer balls were held within it for the delectation of local people and visitors alike. Not far from where it stood, and built into the fabric of the Pier, is a building of rather shed-like appearance with three tall windows inserted on the seaward side (there were also three much narrower ones, of identical height— not visible here—occupying what seems to be the space between the first one and the second). This was a wooden shelter, seated on the inside, for the amenity and comfort of users of the Pier, previously referred to in the **Coastal Scenes** section, in connection with the photograph showing the salvaging of a wreck.

Following the disaster which befell the Reading Room, construction of the South Pier Pavilion began in 1888 and, while there may appear to be little (if any) evidence of building activity in this shot, closer scrutiny suggests that this may not be the case. Even though the photograph's background is faint, it is possible to discern two structures of some kind rising above the level of the wall of the Pier. The nearer of them is directly in line with the North Pierhead's lighthouse, while its companion sits between this lighthouse and the one located on the end of the South Pier. Could these be the western and eastern extremities of the Pavilion, in the earlier stages of its construction? Whatever the case, the photograph itself is obviously one of WRS's earlier Lowestoft studies—of similar date to the second view of Ness Point (1888), which featured in the **Coastal Scenes** section much earlier on.

The main focus of the scene here is the beach, with novelty pony and donkey rides well to the fore—visually as well as in terms of novelty attraction—and the time of day would seem to be about noon, if the length of people's shadows is anything to go by. Perhaps that is why the bowler-hatted gentleman, seated on the sand in the left foreground, appears to be contemplating what lies underneath the white cloth spread over his lap. Is he about to eat his lunch? The man just behind him, wearing a boater, is obviously on the move, but what he is carrying can't be made out. And what the bonneted woman, nearest the camera, is looking down at over the Esplanade's wall is anyone's guess. Just beyond her, and seated on the beach (or on the near-buried section of the wall's curving lower section), close to one of the two signs visible, is another female. She seems to be engaged in some kind of artistic task, making a sketch or drawing perhaps of the activity taking place before her.

Further removed, in the middle ground to the right of centre, some adventurous boys can be seen standing on the timbers of a breakwater or groyne of some kind, while others are visible in the left-hand sector of the frame sitting or standing on the outer timbering of the Pier itself—along with one or two adults. A perfect place, really, for catching the sun on such a day. Then there are the tents (two or three of them), right in the middle of the photograph. Are they there, perhaps, to sell food to people? Shellfish, maybe, including locally caught shrimps. And brown ones in Lowestoft, of course! Not the pink variety, sold further up the coast in Great Yarmouth—which, in any case, were *prawns*.

A scene of relaxation and enjoyment, then, for all those people, young and old—even for the two men (one standing and one sitting) on the upper level of the flint-faced promenade wall, engaged in conversation perhaps with a third one almost hidden by the sign-board. They appear to be wearing working clothes rather than the smarter holiday garb of everyone else (one of them having a nautical cap, of some kind) and may perhaps have walked over from something they were engaged in elsewhere just to have a look at the bank holiday activity. It is noticeable that the people involved in this (with more men and boys immediately visible than women) seem to be wearing clothes of less elegance—for want of a word—than those in the following photograph. That was taken in August, at the height of the holiday season. This one was shot at Whitsun, which falls either in May or June. Can it be that the public holiday here (which was for everyone) has attracted a largely working-class clientèle, keen to take full advantage of a day's break from routine? Whereas, the people in the next scene, being better off financially, could afford to pick and choose when they visited the seaside.

However, even though enjoyment on the sands is everyone's aim, the world of maritime endeavour is there to be seen in the masts of shipping showing above the wall of the Pier and in the twin funnels of a GER paddle-tug moored up in the Yacht Basin—to say nothing of the Trawl Market's roof-line and The Mount lookout-tower, in the distance.

56. South Pier & Beach

A similar location to that of the previous picture is on view here, but with the South Pier Pavilion dominating the middle ground. This photograph being taken the year after it had opened. The quality of the print is marred by fading of the image over much of the area covered, but it is still of interest. A bandstand can be seen in front of the Pavilion and better definition would give the gentle ogee curve of its roof more visual impact and also show more clearly the onion-shaped cupola surmounting it. This being a feature perhaps borrowed from the Brighton Pavilion. The high timber wall along the western section of the Pier, on its southern side, is hardly visible here (the previous photograph shows it much more clearly) and would hide anyone walking the

August 22nd 1892

planking of the deck, but quite a number of people are visible in front of Pavilion and Bandstand, as well as on the open part of the Pier down as far as its end. And, just to the right of the Pavilion, the shadowy outlines of sails show that a smack is leaving the harbour to go trawling.

Again, as with the previous image and commentary, it is the beach itself which takes most of the reader's attention and there is an impressively high level of holiday use in evidence here if the number of people on the sands is anything to go by—though there is no one sitting along the woodwork of the Pier, as in the previous picture, and no young lads standing on the breakwater. There are, however, a few children here and there, paddling at the water's edge. Looking closely at the attire of both adults and children, it would seem that most (if not all) of them are from what might be described as the comfortably-off "middling orders" of society. Right from the beginning, Peto's model resort aimed at attracting that particular social level and, in doing so, it was continuing what had started in the town nearly 100 years before—but a mile or so away, to the north. The High Street area of Lowestoft (as it might conveniently be described by Peto's time) was a much older area of settlement, dating back to the first half of the 14th century, and it had also had its time of local high fashion, during the second half of the 18th century and the earlier decades of the 19th.

It had all begun during the 1760s, with the building of an assembly-room annex at the *Queen's Head* inn (this stood on the south side of Tyler's Lane—now, Compass Street—backing on to the yard of its near-neighbour and rival, *The Crown*), which was a sure sign of the growing "politeness" of towns, both large and small, all over England. This was followed, not long afterwards, by the formation of a book-club and then, in 1768, bathing-machines were introduced to the North Beach (modelled on those in use at Margate) and "taking the waters" became the thing to do for people so disposed and able to afford both the time and money to do it. And, as if this were not enough, the town was able to start and sustain its own soft-paste porcelain factory, which was in production from 1757 to c. 1800—the third longest-lived of all such enterprises after those at Derby and Worcester. One of the factory's leading decorators, Richard Powles, produced a number of fine ink-and-wash sketches of late 18th century Lowestoft and its attractions—perhaps the most evocative of which is a wonderful panoramic view across the Denes, looking towards the town. People are seen "perambulating" there, in the manner that the Revd. James Woodforde, Norfolk clergyman and diarist, did when he paid a visit on 5 April 1786 (accompanied by a nephew) and was highly impressed with what he saw.

Even one leading member of the aristocracy, Charles Sloane (third Baron Cadogan), was sufficiently taken with Lowestoft to have a holiday residence built there, on the top of the cliff, in 1789—something which was deemed newsworthy enough to merit publication in *The Norfolk Chronicle* of 7 November 1789 and 10 July 1790. It is still standing where raised and is now No. 3 High Street. Twenty years or so after this, in 1812, the Fisher family built one of their Norfolk and Suffolk market-town theatres in Bell Lane (later, Crown Street and, now, Crown Street West), to replace a converted fish-house in Blue Anchor Lane (now Duke's Head Street). It, too, is still standing, though converted to flats after serving for many years as a community hub known as *Crown Street Hall*. And, to round everything off culturally, the first two decades of the 19th century also saw the construction of a medicinal bath-house, using local spring water, which welled out in various places along the face of the cliff, as well as at its base. There were two of them, in fact—the first one being built in 1809, followed by a larger replacement in 1824 which remained in use until about the end of the century. Both stood close to what is now the junction of Hamilton Road with Whapload Road.

Thus, Samuel Morton Peto was but one part (albeit of great significance) of an ongoing process in Lowestoft's development as a holiday venue. And the scene here, itself, is exactly the same: part of the late Victorian phase of its overall existence. Reference has already been made to the style and quality of the clothing worn by the people using the beach, this particular day, and there are other things also deserving of comment. The number of parasols, for instance, being used by women to protect them from the heat and glare of the sun; a perambulator, with its hood up, in the middle of the frame, just a little way up from the bottom; and an early pair of deck-chairs in use, just a bit further along to the right (these had only been manufactured in England since 1886—in Macclesfield, of all places). Most interesting of all, perhaps, is a food-vendor or seller of novelties, with a long tray slung around his neck, standing about a third of the way in from the left (on a vertical line down from the bandstand). "What's in the tray?" you ask. The writer's suggestion is shrimps!

15. View of Esplanade from South Pier (tide in)

The eye is immediately taken, in this view, by the bowler-hatted man occupying the bottom right-hand corner of the shot. Was WRS so restricted in getting his photograph of the Esplanade and beach that he had to include him in the frame? Did he, perhaps, ask him to move? Or was it someone he knew, who was included to give an added dimension to the photograph? It certainly does this, even though the person is a little out of focus through being so close to the camera. Not as much, it has to be said, as two other, incomplete figures, one of them apparently wearing a very large top hat (an illusion, surely) and the other poring over a newspaper or magazine of some kind. Immediately behind all three of them can be seen the termination of the high wooden wall of the western section of the South Pier (from where this view was taken), on its southern side.

Obviously, the main focus here is meant to be on the South Beach and Esplanade, both of which are busy. The limited area of the former, available for those occupying it, shows that the tide is in (and quite a high one, at that) and the upper part of the breakwater is only just visible above the water. Close scrutiny shows that the level of the sand is quite high against the wall of the Esplanade and a number of tents, or booths, are plain to see on the right-hand side of the picture—food-stalls, perhaps, or ones which had items of interest for visitors. The four-storey *Royal Hotel* rises impressively behind them, Lowestoft's premier place to stay, almost certainly designed by J.L. Clemence (rather than John Thomas)—as were the row of large three-storey sea-front *villas* stretching southwards. Their command of the promenade was two-fold, both in terms of physical occupation of the space and of the view to be had from each one of them, eastwards, out over the waves. Three sets of composite chimney-stacks are visible between the hotel and the first of the villas and these, of course, belong to Marine Parade—the terrace described at the time of its construction as consisting

Lowestoft Esplanade, from Pier.

of "excellent second-rate houses". It is not difficult to work out the thinking which lay behind this particular description!

It will not go unnoticed that the Esplanade's flagstaff (in front of the *Royal Hotel*) is flying the red cross of St. George, with the Union Jack as an inset in the top left-hand quarter, Could this be 23 April, then—the feast-day of the patron saint of England? Use of a perpetual calendar shows two years set within the known, dated time-frame of WRS's Lowestoft photographs (1887-92) when this fell on a Saturday—1887 and 1892. Perhaps it was the latter of the two, as other images within the collection have this particular year recorded, whereas the former appears just the once: the earliest dated image of all—a view of Ness Point, which featured in the **Coastal Scenes** section. Or is it perhaps the preceding weekend, which was Easter? The people seen on both the beach and the Esplanade are too far away to ascertain the nature of the clothes they're wearing, but April can be a chilly month and it doesn't look particularly sunny here, with a fair breeze blowing if the set of the flag is anything to go by. Significantly, perhaps, hardly anyone is in the sea, paddling—except for three of four children between the third and fourth villas (as seen in the image) and maybe a few more further along. The only thing really occupying the water (which may be too small and indistinct to see here) is a solitary herring gull, which is riding a wavelet a short distance from the Pier, at about a 30° angle from the elbow of the bowler-hatted gentleman, with whom this commentary began—and, now, ends.

20. View of Esplanade from South Pier (another day, tide out)

Another day is presented here, with nothing flying from the Esplanade's flagpole on this occasion, and with the tide much further out than in the previous photograph. The buildings on show are exactly the same, though slightly less is seen of the *Royal Hotel* and a lot less of the sea-front villas, with only four of the latter visible. *White's Directory of Suffolk* (1872) informs the reader that the hotel was built in 1848-9 and that it had eighty bedrooms, with hot and cold baths available. There were billiard rooms inside, as well as "spacious and superbly furnished dining and drawing rooms". It was, in every way, a building worthy of its creator's vision.

Activity on the beach in front of it, and further along, would seem to say that the summer has arrived, as lots of children can be seen playing and enjoying themselves in the shallows, and the left forearm of the person resting on the edge of the South Pier's parapet (barely in frame, in the bottom right-hand corner of the image) suggests that he or she is watching them. What looks as if it may be over-exposure of the shot diminishes its effectiveness, but not to the point of failing to show the level of the sand against the Esplanade's wall which, as in the previous view, is quite high, especially to the left of centre. A figure standing in line with the end of the first villa (as the print makes it appear) suggests that the promenade's surface is somewhere between waist and shoulder high.

The chimney stacks of the Marine Parade houses show much more strongly here and the vegetation seen growing to the rear of the *Royal Hotel* and the villas provides quite a contrast to the uncompromising outlines of the buildings. The scale of these structures is impressive (as it was meant to be) and so is their vertical and horizontal geometry, with the low-profile roof-lines perfectly angled to create a sense of harmony and order. Two of the hotel's ground-floor bays have sun-screening in place and it is just possible to make out a balcony running along the façade on the level above. An engraving of the building, dating from the 1850s and made not long after it was constructed, shows this to have been of metal fabrication with each panel between the uprights having diamond patterning. The northern, three-bay elevation is equally impressive, with rusticated stonework at ground-floor level and elaborate brickwork and stone quoining of both outer bays, which project slightly from the middle one and have low-profile, triangular broken-pediments to crown them. The whole of this important and impressive building was demolished in 1973, its heyday long gone and, unfortunately, with no obvious use to ensure its survival. Such has been the fate of many a structure, both in Lowestoft and in other towns and cities throughout the country.

58. Beach, *Royal Hotel* & Esplanade from South Pier (1)

A similar view to the previous one is shown here—except that a good deal more of the sea-front villas is visible and the Esplanade's flagstaff has moved to the other side of the *Royal Hotel*. And what a difference in the level of the beach! This has dropped by six feet or more and not only are two of the rounded buttresses of the esplanade plainly visible, but a shelter has been installed between them. It has been established that this particular date was a Monday (see the previous section, last photograph but one) and it was obviously a very busy one. And hot! All seven bays of the *Royal Hotel's* ground-floor have sun-screens in place on the walkway below the balcony—the latter being clearer to see in this shot than in its predecessor—and many of the villas have both ground- and first-floor windows similarly shielded by awnings. A substantial number of children are enjoying a paddle in the sea and at least one boy is climbing over the fully visible wooden breakwater, with another one about to follow suit. The beach, as a whole, is thronged with people—young and old alike—and so is the Esplanade, with both of the buttresses (decorative features, as much as structural ones) serving to provide seating convenient for sitting down and taking a breather.

August 22nd 1892

It might be thought that the sheer numbers seen indicate that this is August bank holiday. The introduction, in 1871, of a public holiday for employees of the Bank of England (and for those of other banks) led to the name "bank holiday" being applied generally to those Mondays given over to a break from work. The August one was intended, originally—among other things—to give men working in banks the opportunity to enjoy watching or playing a game of cricket. But that fell on the first Monday of the month right up until 1971—when it was changed to the last. The 22nd was the fourth Monday in August 1892, so there must be other explanations. One offered in the commentary relating to the photograph of the lifeboats, in the previous section, was the possibility of the annual Regatta being held later in the week.

The drop in the level of the beach, noted above, would have been caused by the erosive action of the sea. There must have been a notably high winter tide (or tides) at some stage, which had carried a lot of the sand away. This happens all the way along the Norfolk and Suffolk coastline, and Lowestoft is no exception. This very area of the South Beach suffered serious damage not so many years ago and both rebuilding of parts of the Esplanade and putting in rock protection (large lumps of Norwegian granite) have been carried out. Not a great deal further to the south, the beach just beyond the Claremont Pier (built 1902-3 and therefore post-dating WRS's connection with the town) builds up significantly, at times, and has to be redistributed. Thus, this particular shot is not only a record of a particular time and place, but one which serves also to remind us today of natural forces which are ongoing in their effect (for good or bad) on the environment.

The historically recent damage done to the Esplanade and adjacent beach-area revealed just how well engineered the former is, by exposing lower parts of the structure and revealing the quality of its brickwork (high-fired stock, to counter the effect of permanent damp). It serves a dual purpose—the original function being to provide a sea-wall which would enable Peto's resort both to be built and to stand against the waves. Once that had been achieved, then putting in the roadways and raising the terraces and the grand hotel could proceed. The area chosen was beach and low coastal heath, vulnerable to high tides, and any development necessitated digging down through the light, geological surface deposits of sand and shingle to firmer levels beneath (piling of the harbour's piers would have had to have done the same). And digging was something which Peto knew all about. He built railways and employed a large force of navvies, some of whom would have been deployed to work on his Lowestoft projects. It would be an exaggeration to claim that as much building exists below ground as is seen above, but in a sense it is true, because without sound footings what stood above would not have endured. Matthew 7. 26 & 27 tells us that a house built on sand will not stand. Peto knew that and dug down, deep, and what he created has now stood for 170 years.

55. Beach, *Royal Hotel* & Esplanade from South Pier (2)

This particular photograph is the natural opposite of No. 56 above, providing us with a view of the South Beach and Esplanade taken from the South Pier, as opposed to the South Pier and Beach taken from the Esplanade. It gives a similar aspect to others already seen, but with much more of the Pier itself visible, including its entrance-area, with those two distinctive kiosks. The length of wooden wall (screening is perhaps a more appropriate word) on the seaward side is a prominent feature and it had been installed, at some stage, to prevent people being splashed by wave impact on the breakwater below—this structure also being plain to see. Three large pennants, suspended between two flagstaffs, are prominent in the middle ground and one of them has wrapped itself around the line. There are a lot more people on the beach and Esplanade than there are on this part of the Pier, but at least five parasols are set against the sun and the two gentlemen, walking along together in the immediate foreground, are certainly dressed in lighter clothing appropriate for such hot weather—the one wearing the striped blazer particularly. Both of them carry reading material, with the left-hand one reading a magazine or brochure of some sort. The one figure definitely not affected by the high temperature (as far as can be seen) is the young girl in a white dress, seen running down the boardwalk—reminding one, perhaps, of those vibrant seaside maidens, painted at this very time by Philip Wilson Steer further down the coast, at Walberswick.

August 22nd 1892

WRS must have been standing on the first-floor balcony of the South Pier Pavilion to have taken this shot, its walkway canopied over on the eastern and western ends. There is much to see that has been commented on already: the busy beach, the breakwater and the children it has attracted, the wall of the Esplanade with its buttresses and the shelter placed between them, and the sun-screening measures adopted at the hotel and villas. But that's not all. The wider view than previous ones, northwards, allows the first of the statues of the sea-god Triton (which stood at intervals along the Esplanade) to be noted. He who was the son of Poseidon and Amphitrite, customarily depicted as half-man and half-fish, and who is shown here in Lowestoft wrestling with a serpentine sea-monster (the figure carries a Grade II listing as being of architectural merit). He is mounted on a pillar and can be detected, in the middle distance, between the central and right-hand pennants hanging from their overhead line. Further removed, and on the right-hand edge of the frame, the tower and spire of St. John's Church are visible—the place of worship built specifically for the population of the new seaside suburb.

Best of all though, surely, is what is to be seen in the extreme bottom right-hand corner of the photograph: someone in a canoe, paddling along in the Yacht Basin. Was WRS aware of him? Or was it just a happy accident that he happened to be there when the shutter dropped? If the posture of the people leaning on the inner rail of Pier is anything to go by, they might well have been watching what he was doing.

44. South Pier & Pavilion

This is undoubtedly the best study of the South Pier Pavilion in this section, simply because WRS is focused on the building itself. It is extremely well proportioned, with slender balcony supports and their curvilinear arch-braces bringing a delicacy of touch to the whole of the ground-floor level. The uprights then carry on through, in reduced form, to the roof above the upper walkway, which is itself of subtle concavity in assembled sections made of either lead or copper sheeting. Here we see Victorian metalwork at its finest, with the cast-iron pillars and capitals, the arch-braces, and both the upper and lower guard-rails demonstrating foundry work of the highest quality. The previous image shown was captured from the western end of the Pavilion. Here, we are looking the eastern one, which gives an equally good idea of the vantage-point WRS had round the other side. It is hard to say what time of day this is, because the Pier is almost deserted and there are very few people on what little there is to be seen of the beach. Early morning or mid-late evening would seem to be the best guesses available. Furthermore, the sun does not appear to be shining, so perhaps the sole umbrella seen indicates rain or drizzle. The sun-screens are still in place on the ground-floor of the *Royal Hotel*, but they would probably have stayed put during a hot spell, anyway. The total length of the South Pier was a quarter of a mile and the linearity of its boarded deck is sufficient here (in the almost complete absence of people) to give a real sense of length and distance—the Pavilion being located halfway along from the entrance.

There is evidence available, from other images in this section featuring the building, to show that this photograph was taken in 1891—the year that it opened. Both of the pictures dated 22 August 1892 (nos. 55 & 58) have the Esplanade's flagstaff on the left-hand side of the *Royal Hotel*, whereas two other, undated ones (nos. 15 & 20) have it to the right—as does this one (no. 44), though no flag is flying from it. Therefore, the Pavilion was in its very first year of use, going on to serve as a key part of Lowestoft's holiday attractions, to both visitors and local residents alike, up until the outbreak of the Second World War. A lone figure on the balcony is looking out to sea, the lady with the umbrella has already been noted, and three or four more people in the distance are seen to be leaving. The only other presence is the object lying in the middle of the Pier's decking, which no amount of magnification and rotation has managed to identify. With comparatively little to comment upon, in the way of human activity, the Pavilion becomes the focus of attention and is able to make its own statement regarding its value both as a building in its own right and as an essential part of the seaside environment.

It sustained damage during World War Two and was demolished in about 1954. A new Pavilion took its place, which was opened by the Duke of Edinburgh in May 1956. This was very much a building to suit and to reflect the times—a good, mid-century, Modernist structure, with a gently rounded roof and a bold, rectangular, six-storey, seaward-side observation block rising beside it. Constructed of steel and glass, the latter had its top level as an open-air viewing platform, providing a fine command of its surrounds, both out to sea and inland. It was designed by Edward Skipper & Associates, of Norwich—the said Edward being the son of G.J. (George) Skipper who had designed the RN&SYC headquarters over fifty years before. In tandem with this new development, a miniature-railway line was constructed along the whole length of the Pier. Alterations carried out during 1974-5 saw the removal of the observation block and shortening of the shoreward end of the building. Further alterations and developments have taken place since, leaving nothing of the Skipper building remaining and having only the Family Entertainment Centre at the west end of the Pier as the sole attraction.

During the 1960s, both the South Pier and the *Royal Hotel* became important local venues for live popular music. To name all the bands and individuals who gave performances would produce an interesting study all of its own, but it is perhaps worth noting that Little Richard himself appeared at the *Royal Hotel* in May 1964, while the Yardbirds featured there the following year, in March. The Rolling Stones made appearances at both places—the *Royal Hotel* in September 1963 and the South Pier Pavilion in January 1964. Further down the line, local legend has it that, in May 1978, Dire Straits played to about fifteen people at the South Pier, while on tour, and thought about calling it a day. *Sultans of Swing* was having no success with the listening public and things, generally, were not going well. Not all that long afterwards, in January 1979, the record was re-issued and met with success in the USA, before returning home to the United Kingdom—and the rest, as they say, is history!

Pier and Reading Room. Lowestoft

54. Yacht Basin & Tug *Imperial*

The last view but one in this section shows the whole of the Yacht Basin, with the South Pier Pavilion looming in the middle distance. It is just about possible to make out the lighthouses of both Pierheads, further removed and in the centre of the frame—the North one, on the left, better defined than its companion. In front of the Pavilion (as it appears, to the reader) a line of yachts are moored up to the dolphins, while just beyond the gardens and almost in the middle of the frame a white *lugsail* set on its yard can be seen, belonging obviously, to some sailing craft which is laid against the west wall of the basin. On the left, the GER paddle-tug *Imperial* is tied up at the north jetty and, on the other side of it, in the bridge channel, is another of the harbour's work-horses, its single funnel showing faintly. It does not appear to be a paddle-steamer, which means that it was probably the screw-driven vessel *Resolute*. Beyond the *Imperial*, another small sailing vessel (with large white lugsail, of *lateen* proportions) is seen entering the basin—the total spread of its canvas fully extended.

The dominant feature in this photograph is the garden-space in front of the camera, which WRS seems to have chosen as his main subject—though he probably hoped for better definition in the scene's background. Obviously, it is not possible to identify any particular species of plant in a black-and-white photograph of this period (unless possessing a really expert eye), but the layout seems to consist of a combination of shrubs and hardy perennials—all of which would have had to withstand challenging winds in the winter and a high level of salt in the air all year round. Good quality woodwork may be seen in the palings of the perimeter fence, which are attached to horizontal bars at the top and bottom and have supporting wooden posts, each with a nicely carved finial on the top. And within this barrier, part of a serpentine pathway can be seen working its way round within the raised and planted areas, providing anyone choosing to walk along it with a small and temporary environment completely different from that which lay outside.

As always, the human figures in the scene add greatly to its interest—whether this is as individuals, as couples, or in groups. Furthest from the camera, are four men standing on the jetty near *Imperial*, while a fifth is about to join them or is just leaving. The next two are definitely leaving, the one on the left wearing a white calico slop, or *jumper*. If the shot is magnified, a boy can be seen walking just in front of him. At the western edge of the Yacht Basin, in front of a post in the quayside (is he leaning back against it?) a man in a white slop seems to be studying the tug, while over to his right a group of five or six men are engaged in conversation. To the right of them, a single individual stands, half-seeming to be part of the little company.

Nearer to the camera, a group of four men of nautical appearance (on the style of the three caps and single bowler) stand at the corner of the fence, definitely leaning against it and having a chat. Is it possible that they might have belonged to the *Imperial's* crew? The gentleman who has just walked past them, white-bearded and with a walking-stick, certainly didn't—though it is not possible to say anything more than that, other than that he seems older than anyone else on view. The two men seen standing together between him and the two-wheeled trap being driven past are certainly having a "head-to-head", with the one nearest the camera wearing yet another untanned calico jumper. To the rear of them, looking very much as if he's heading for the garden-area's fence, is a man in a lightweight suit, wearing a boater. He's carrying something in his right hand, but it's not possible to make out what it is. Already at the fence, and walking along it side by side just beyond the light, covered wagon which is passing by, two more people are to be seen—one of whom (a woman) is carrying a parasol. Beyond them, and more or less aligned with the necks of the two horses, another woman dressed in dark clothes is walking along. The length of the shadows cast by both people and vehicles suggests a time around mid-afternoon or a little later.

Two things remain with no comment made concerning them. One is the handcart left upended against the picket fence, between the bearded gentleman and him of the light suit and boater. Where are the shafts? Taken out and stashed away somewhere for safe-keeping because, if left in place on an unattended vehicle, someone could easily have walked off with it. The other is the notice board which is seen behind the covered wagon and which stood just within the garden-area. In another view similar to the one depicted here (reproduced elsewhere), but much clearer and more sharply defined, the lettering at the top of it can be read. It says H. CLARKE FRUITERER & FLORIST, advertising a business located in the main part of town, in Milton Road—probably that occupied by the Sansom family at a much later date.

53. Esplanade Approach & Royal Plain

In a sense, this is the other half of the previous photograph—but not taken on the same day, and probably without any intention on WRS's part that it should be regarded as the second of two components. No shadows are cast here and no parasols are raised against the heat and glare of the sun. In fact, there seems to have been a little rain at some point, if the patches of moisture on the ground are anything to go by (they're not really large enough to rate as puddles). The southern end of the garden-space clearly shows the pathway located between the raised areas of planting on either side and the seaside shelter at the end has people sitting within it. The building seen beyond the garden is clubhouse of the RN&SYC and just to the right of it is one of the two entry-booths to the South Pier—the decorative nature of its roof detectable even at a distance. People are seen standing at, or walking along, the edge of the Esplanade and the first sea-front representation of Triton (by John Thomas) wrestling with the sea monster stands out clearly. So does the flagstaff, previously noted in this particular location in Nos. 15, 20 & 44. A number of horse-drawn carriages are seen waiting to take passengers on board for a tour of the Esplanade and other parts of the town (and also, perhaps, to see places beyond the confines of Lowestoft), and the whole scene has a sense of human activity and purpose about it—but without the sheer number of people who are present in the majority of the other images presented in this section.

On the extreme right of the picture, the edge of the *Royal Hotel* can be seen and, in fact, the area where it stood was known as the Royal Plain after the hotel itself—a name which continues in use, right down to the present day. WRS had obviously managed to find himself a suitable position above ground-level, to take this shot (and its predecessor also) but exactly how must remain a matter of conjecture. It seems likely to have been from the first floor of the *Harbour Hotel* (J.L. Clemence again), which he might well have patronised while visiting his father and which was suitably located to give him both the angles required. He might even have stayed there, of course, when he came to Lowestoft. It wasn't as grand (or expensive) as the *Royal Hotel*, but it was of a good standard nevertheless and able to provide suitable accommodation for a man of WRS's social position. It was also located no more than about 150 yards from 16 Marine Parade. Both it and the *Royal*, as well as the sea-front villas, would have constituted the first phase of Peto's resort development, after construction of the sea wall and probably date, therefore, from the mid-late 1840s. All of them have Clemence's characteristic facades, with shallow roof-lines, low-profile gables and cased brick window-surrounds, creating an overall simplicity of appearance which brings a pleasing sense of restraint to the whole layout. The photographs seen above, in this section, numbered 20, 58 and 55 serve to demonstrate this and make their own unequivocal statement of the man's competence.

Whatever the photographer's exact location, it certainly led to a fine study of a late Victorian gas lamp! On the extreme left of the frame, a man is seen pushing some kind of two-wheeled cart carrying what appears to be a dustbin and work-box of some kind. He is also wearing a protective apron under his jacket and has either completed some kind of maintenance or repair work somewhere or is on his way to carry some out—possibly both. It is doubtful whether the dustbin contains what the horses standing on Royal Plain might have produced. That would have been swept up and disposed of, at the end of the day. Across the other side of the image, stands a covered two-wheel handcart, which seems to function as a movable food-stall—though without anyone giving it custom at the time the photograph was taken.

Right in the middle of the frame, another man is carrying a booth of some sort—perhaps on his way home from the beach. Although the general shape is roughly the same, it seems a little too lacking in depth to be a Punch and Judy stand and nothing else seems to be associated with it. Unless the female figure on the pathway, next to the garden's fence, has things connected on the barrow which she is pushing. And then there are the two people following the man, one of them definitely a woman and the other hard to determine because of the head and shoulders being obscured by some kind of white cloth or wrapping. And is that a shoeshine boy at work, on the pavement-edge immediately behind them? It looks as if it could be—but without the necessary certainty that it is. There's a good deal in this shot which creates speculation, and that's what helps to make it so interesting. The two children, for instance, in the middle distance, standing apart, not far from the group of people on the pavement (two girls, by the look of it), with the one nearer the kerb holding a small bucket. A discussion seems to be taking place between them—perhaps about what is contained in the bucket?

And so, the photographic record which William Rayson Smith made of Lowestoft comes to an end—leaving us all wanting to see more. And also, perhaps, wishing either that more of his work had been devoted to the town or, if it had, regretting that that it has not survived to remain available for us to look at and consider what it might tell us about a bygone age.

Lowestoft

THAT OTHER PLACE!

Most local people (and perhaps others who live further afield) will know something of the rivalry between Lowestoft and the town of Great Yarmouth, which lasted for all of 300 years, from the middle of the 14th century to the middle of the 17th, and then continued for another 300 or more at a less intense level. It all hinged, originally, on Great Yarmouth's assertion of its maritime rights relating to seaborne trade, particularly the catching, processing and sale of herrings during the autumn fishing season—this pelagic species being the great staple of the town's economy. By having the so-called Statute of Herrings passed in its favour in the year 1357, Yarmouth was given control of the seas within seven *leucae* [leagues] of its harbour—a privilege confirmed in 1372 in a re-granting of its municipal charter. In both of these official pronouncements the length of the *leuca* or league (a flexible unit of measurement, which could be one, two or even three miles) and the point from which it was to be taken were not stated—conveniently, or inconveniently, depending on how the matter was regarded.

Great Yarmouth argued for the *leuca* to be a two-mile length and for the start of the measurement to be made from its harbour mouth. At the time, this was much further to the south, off Gunton, and therefore not so very far from reaching Lowestoft itself. This was because a long sand-spit prevented direct access to the Norfolk town's harbour and necessitated passage along an inner channel which silted up regularly. Lowestoft, of course, contested this interpretation of the legislation, claiming that the *leuca* meant a mile in length, and no more, and that the stipulated distance should be measured from the quayside in Yarmouth, where goods were landed. The arguments dragged on and on, with claim and counter-claim regularly being made in Parliament by each community using MPs supporting its case, until a final, definitive judgement was made in May 1662 stating that a *leuca* was a mile only in length and that the distance of seven such units was to be measured from the base of the crane on Crane Quay in the heart of Great Yarmouth itself—close to the present-day Town Hall. The measurement was duly carried out, with verifiers present, and an oak post set up on the beach at Corton, somewhere to the north of the access-point now known as Tramp's Alley (Lopham Score, at the time—later, Locum Hole), just over a mile to the north of Lowestoft parish boundary.

The rivalry between the two towns continued, of course, but it became increasingly a matter of civic posturing rather than legal wrangling, eventually developing into local banter of the kind existing all over England between nearby, rival communities. Great Yarmouth citizens referred to the good people of Lowestoft as "pea-bellies"—a reference to the alleged consumption of the seeds of the sea pea (*Lathyrus japonicus*), which grew wild on the Denes and which served to demonstrate the poverty-stricken nature of the town and its inhabitants by their having to resort to such a diet. Lowestoft retaliated by referring to people living in Yarmouth as "rednecks"—probably as an indication of general uncouthness on their part, as well as a tendency to be opinionated. It can't have been connected with the red flannel neckerchiefs, or wrappers (*wroppers*, in local parlance), adopted by fishermen as a protection against chafing of the neck by the rough working-garments worn at sea, because the crew members of both ports used them.

Be that as it may, and somewhat enigmatically, WRS has left us with only two photographs taken in Great Yarmouth. Both are of well-known landmarks in the town, but there is no indication of why there is not more of a record of his visit. Great Yarmouth is a place full of interest, where a man of his skill would have had a field-day taking pictures. Did he, in fact, take more? And if so, why haven't they survived? Both the Town Hall and St. Nicholas's Church are some distance apart, with the famous Tolhouse, for instance, quite close to the former and the Fishermen's Hospital within easy distance of the latter. Each would have made an excellent study, in its own right. Yet neither of them has been handed down. Furthermore, he wouldn't have captured everything that Yarmouth had to show in a single day (the town being too extensive in area), and the following list may serve to illustrate what was there to be photographed. Along the sea-front, there would have been any number of beach scenes available, as well as a good selection of the more imposing buildings—the Jetty, the Wellington Pier, the Britannia Pier and the Nelson Monument. In the built-up part of town, there was the Naval Hospital, the Town Wall, the South-east Tower, the Greyfriars ruins, the Rows, and the Market Place. And, finally, along the river, there was the Bridge, shipping of all kinds (both fishing vessels and merchant craft) and the magnificence of South Quay itself, which Daniel Defoe had declared to be the finest wharf in Europe, apart from the one at Marseilles, in the first volume of his *A Tour Thro' the Whole Island of Great Britain* (1724).

However, we have to take things as they are, not as we would like them to be. So, it is now time to consider the last two images in this collection of his work.

45. Great Yarmouth Town Hall

Town Hall. Yarmouth

This, the town's civic headquarters, was designed by the architect, J.B. Pearce of Norwich, and built 1882-3, so it was a comparatively new structure when photographed by WRS. It had superseded a Georgian Town Hall on the site, and before that, the town's ancient Tolhouse a few hundred yards away, with its 13th century origins as prestigious merchant's house and its modifications thereafter into a combination of court-house, gaol and place of receipt for payment of the customs due on cargoes both coming into Yarmouth and leaving it. That venerable building then changed use and became a museum—a function which it retains to this day. The red-brick Town Hall seen here is absolutely typical of its time, both in terms of scale and appearance, and it remains an impressive structure even now. As a town of regional importance and with some degree of national status attaching to it, Great Yarmouth needed (and had to have) a town hall able to fulfil its role in local government and to make a visual statement of civic confidence and pride.

What we see has everything required of a centre of local administration: sufficient interior space to carry out its day-to-day business and an exterior intended to impress. In this case, one with bold fenestration (especially on the first-floor level), good vertical and horizontal lines, decorative cornices, swags and balustrades on the top level, deep roof-lines, and an ornamental clock-tower with cupola. The clock itself gives a time of 12.45 p.m. (a quarter to one, if preferred). And if any particular style has to be attached to the edifice, pseudo-Queen Anne might suit, for the Victorians never minded about mixing their architectural metaphors—something which adds such interest to their buildings and (often) an accompanying eccentricity. Given this attribution, it is probably true to say that the Yarmouth Town Hall owes something to the leading exponent of this style of building, the London architect R.N. ("Norman") Shaw, who used it widely in work carried out in the capital.

Two boys in the foreground (one of them holding what appears to be a box under his left arm) are obviously interested in what WRS is doing—as is the woman standing not far from them, though she must have moved as the shutter dropped to cause such blurring of her person. The seven other people in the frame are all on the move, so there is little that can be said about them. The road to the right of the Town Hall leads on from Hall Quay to South Quay and the river, and that to the left down towards the Tolhouse, with the National Provincial Bank Limited's premises visible on the corner of Hall Quay and Regent Street. The curved area of bollarding in front of it was obviously placed there to prevent vehicles from cutting straight through, rather than following the bend of the road and the rear part of a carriage and one wheel can just be seen going in the opposite direction. It might have been one of the equipages from the sea-front, which took paying passengers for trips around the town—something which is still done today and is very much a feature of the Yarmouth holiday experience.

The physical size of the Town Hall is obviously the dominant feature of this photograph, but it is accentuated by the small number of people present (ten, in all) in the immediate vicinity. A quarter to one, in the middle of the day, close to the bridge and South Quay, as well as to the middle of the built-up residential area. Where is everyone? They can't all be having lunch! Why is there so little human activity in such a usually busy part of town? The answer is to be found in the image which follows.

46. Parish Church of St. Nicholas, Great Yarmouth

St. Nicholas's Church is an architectural gem, of early 12th century origins as part of a Benedictine priory (founded by Herbert de Losinga, Bishop of Norwich), but with many later additions and alterations, all of which help to enhance the building's history and appearance. It probably stands on the site of an earlier place-of-worship recorded in Domesday Book as *qda eccla sci Benedicti*—which translates as "a certain church of Saint Benedict". This either means that it was called St. Benedict's at the time (the likelihood) or that it had been under the control of the Abbey of St. Benet Holm, in the Norfolk parish of Horning, to the north-east of Norwich (Benet being a medieval variant of "Benedict"). This particular foundation was influential in that part of the county which later became known as "Broadland", and its reach would certainly have extended as far as Yarmouth.

The interior of St. Nicholas is some 23,000 square feet in area—a size which has led to it being called "the largest parish church in the country". The writer is not qualified to make a definitive pronouncement on this description, but it is certainly a very large and impressive enclosed space. It can been seen, from the outside, that the building is of cruciform shape, with central tower (plus later, added spire)—a sure sign of Norman origins—and the west end of it is particularly imposing with its triple gables and four elegant polygonal buttresses rising into the air. These buttresses are mirrored in smaller versions on each transept and on the four corners of the tower. The church was burnt out in 1942, following an enemy air-raid on the town, and the work of rebuilding it was carried out during 1957-60 under the supervision of the architect S. Dykes Bower. His restoration was a very successful one, which gave back to the town perhaps its most notable building in terms of historical importance and value as a feature of the urban landscape.

The northern end of Church Plain, seen here, is apparently devoid of any human activity, except for one

St. Nicholas. Yarmouth

small boy looking towards the camera and apparently shading his eyes against the light with his left hand. In this respect, there is even less visible human presence than was evident in the preceding photograph. So, once again, where is everybody? The answer must surely lie in the particular day of the week, on which the picture was taken: Sunday! There was no direct way of getting from Lowestoft to Yarmouth by rail during the 1880s and 90s, so the journey must have been made by road in a horse and trap (or carriage) of some kind. And it would have taken an hour and a half or so, on the road surfaces of the time, to cover the ten miles between the two towns. Great Yarmouth Town Hall would have been the first of the two buildings encountered on crossing the River Yare and, with its clock showing a time of 12.45 p.m., this means that WRS (and whoever he was with, if he was accompanied) must have left Lowestoft round about 11.00 a.m.

Having got his shot of the Town Hall, he would then have probably made his way the half-mile westwards to the Parish Church and taken the photograph seen here. The particular time he was in Great Yarmouth, being that of the midday meal, would partly account for the lack of people being seen in both images, but a further factor was that Sunday was a day of rest for most people, so there was no need for them to be busying themselves in weekday matters. The line of houses next to the church offers a pleasing aspect in terms of the varying styles of build, with contrasting roof-lines and variation in types of window and door-cases. The first complete façade, on the left-hand side of the frame, declares this building to be the premises of W.J. Benns, who was a corn merchant, and a pony in the shafts of a cart can be seen standing outside the shop next door.

Wait a minute! The blinds of Mr. Benns's ground-floor windows are drawn, showing that the business is closed. So, this is confirmation that the day in question is, indeed, the Sabbath! And there's obviously "Sunday trading" of some kind going on (legal or otherwise), because another pony and cart can be seen backed up into the doorway (partially obscured by the cylindrical postbox), with loaded sacks on board—presumably, containing grain. Which means that the animal already noted is waiting for its own cart to be loaded. And was the boy in the photograph perhaps facing in the other direction from the one suggested earlier, with his right hand held up to the back of his head (for whatever reason), looking at what is happening in front of Mr. Benns's premises. There's something in the set of his body, and particularly of his legs, which suggests that this might well have been the case.

Why, oh why, isn't there more of a WRS perspective on Great Yarmouth and its activities! Did he really make the journey, all the way from Lowestoft, just to capture these two particular buildings and their surrounds, and nothing else?

POSTSCRIPT

"Excellent Second-rate House"

16, MARINE PARADE,
LOWESTOFT
The Excellent Freehold
RESIDENCE,
known as No. 16, Marine Parade, Lowestoft, which has been considerably enlarged. Built of White Brick and Covered with Slates, and containing the following accommodation:- On the Top Floor: Two Front Bedrooms (one with Cupboard), Back Bedroom (with Cupboard and Linen Cupboard), Landing (with Linen Cupboard), Back Bedroom with enclosed Washstand and Shelf. On the first floor: Drawing Room with Bay Window and Marble Mantel Piece with 2 recesses, Back Bedroom with 2 Cupboards, Landing, Bath Room with Geyser, Lavatory and W.C. On the ground floor: Entrance Hall, Dining Room with Bay Window and Marble Mantel Piece communicating by Sliding Doors to Breakfast Room having a Marble Mantel Piece and 2 glazed Cupboards, Butler's Pantry with Enamelled Basin, Shelves and Cup-Board. In Basement: Front Kitchen with Range, Cupboards and Dresser, Pantry, Scullery with Range, Copper and Sink, Passage with 2 Store Cupboards, Coal House and W.C., and Garden entrance. At rear: Coal House and Store, Garden with entrance to London Road South. The House, which has an excellent sea view, is in fair repair throughout. Immediate Possession. Particulars and Conditions of Sale may be obtained of the Auctioneers, or of Messrs Lyus & Son, Diss, Norfolk, Vendor's Solicitors.

This advertisement appeared in the *Lowestoft Journal* of 15 March 1919. It has been reproduced in the same columnar format as the original and as closely as possible to it. It was probably placed in the newspaper by Notleys, Auctioneers, House & Estate Agents. Any enlargement of this terraced house must have consisted of buildings added to the back of it and possibly by re-arrangement of certain internal spaces. Perhaps this particular notice of sale was seen by Rosa Norton, who purchased the property from WRS's sister Eliza on 12 May 1919—the latter having already returned to live at Redenhall, in her home-area of South Norfolk. At a selling price of £600 (see the **Preface**, p. 6), the house was £75 cheaper than it had been in 1868. The reason for this is probably to be found in the description of it being "in fair repair throughout"—which suggests that it had things about it requiring attention.

SELECT BIBLIOGRAPHY

Barney, J.,	*The Norfolk Railway: Railway Mania in East Anglia 1834-1862* (Norwich, 2007).
Boxall, J. & D.,	*The Photographs of William Rayson Smith, Volume I: Norfolk and Beyond* (Lowestoft, 2020).
Brooks, C.,	*Lowestoft, Volume 1: A Portrait in Old Picture Postcards* (Market Drayton, 1991).
Butcher, D.,	*The Driftermen* (Reading, 1979).
	The Trawlermen (Reading, 1980).
	Living From the Sea (Reading, 1982).
	Following the Fishing (Newton Abbot, 1987).
	The Ocean's Gift (Norwich, 1995).
	Lowestoft 1550-1580: Development & Change in a Suffolk Coastal Town (Woodbridge, 2008).
	Fishing Talk (Cromer, 2014).
	Medieval Lowestoft: the Origins and Growth of a Suffolk Coastal Community (Woodbridge, 2016).
	The Last Haul (Lowestoft, 2020).
Cherry, P.,	*Victorian Lowestoft* (Lowestoft, 1992).
Cherry, P. & Westgate, T.,	*The Roaring Boys of Suffolk* (Hadleigh, 1970).
Clements P.,	*Lowestoft – 200 Years a Seaside Resort* (Lowestoft, 1994).
Colman, H.,	*Jeremiah James Colman: a Memoir* (London, 1905).
Defoe, D.,	*Tour Through the Eastern Counties* (London, 1724; Ipswich, 1984).
Dyson, J.,	*Business in Great Waters* (London, 1977).
Ecclestone, A.W. (ed.),	*Henry Manship's Great Yarmouth* (Great Yarmouth, 1971).
Elliott, C.,	*Sailing Fishermen in Old Photographs* (Reading, 1978).
Flood, J.,	*List of Fishing Vessels Registered At the Port of Lowestoft* (Lowestoft, 1903).
Freeman, J. & E.,	*Old Lowestoft* (Mauchline, 2009).
Gillingwater, E.,	*An Historical Account of the Ancient Town of Lowestoft* (London, 1790).
Hedges, A.A.C.,	*Yarmouth Is an Antient Town* (Great Yarmouth, 1959).
Higgins, D.,	*The Beachmen* (Lavenham, 1987).
Huke, T.,	*Directory of Lowestoft & Kirkley* (Lowestoft, 1892).
Malster, R.,	*Wherries and Waterways* (Lavenham, 1971).
	Saved From the Sea (Lavenham, 1974).
	Lowestoft East Coast Port (Lavenham, 1982).
	Lowestoft: a Pictorial History (Chichester, 1991).
	Maritime Norfolk, Part Two (Cromer 2013).
	Maritime Suffolk (Cromer, 2017).
Murton, A.E. (ed.),	*Gillingwater's History of Lowestoft* (Lowestoft, 1897).

Neville, J. & Bunn S.,	*Dickleburgh Burston Wood Post Mill* (Internet resource: www.norfolkmills.co.uk, 2014).
Olsen, O.T.,	*The Fisherman's Nautical Almanack* (Grimsby, 1911).
Robb, I.G.,	*Lowestoft: Britain in Old Photographs* (Stroud, 1995).
	Lowestoft Past and Present (Stroud, 2000).
Rose, J.,	*Jack Rose's Lowestoft* (Lowestoft, 1981).
	Jack Rose's Lowestoft Album (Lowestoft, 1983).
	Jack Rose's Lowestoft Scrapbook (Lowestoft, 1988).
	Jack Rose's Lowestoft Life (Lowestoft, 1991).
	Jack Rose's Lowestoft Picture Show (Lowestoft, 1998).
Rose, J. & Parkin, D.,	*The Grit* (Lowestoft, 1997).
	The Grit (updated version – Halesworth, 2019).
Vaughn, A.,	*Samuel Morton Peto* (Shepperton, 2006).
Ward, J.,	*The Iron Bridge* (Lowestoft, 2004).
Ward Lock & Co. Ltd.,	*Illustrated Guide Book: Lowestoft & District* (London, 1937).
White, W.,	*History, Gazetteer and Directory of Suffolk* (Sheffield, 1844).
White, W.,	*History, Gazetteer and Directory of Suffolk* (Sheffield, 1872).
Wren, W.,	*Ports of the Eastern Counties* (Lavenham, 1976).

INDEX

People

Commercial Enterprises & Other Organisations

Lowestoft & Its Locality

Foreign Locations

Maritime Areas

Fishing Vessels & Other Craft

You may also like

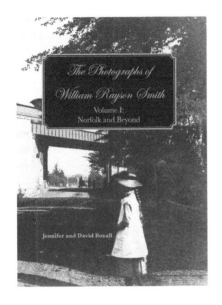

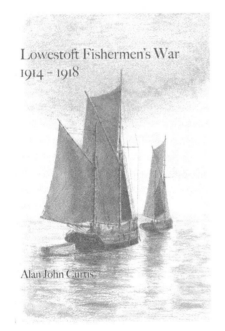

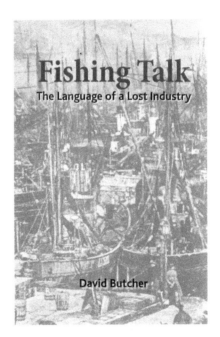

available from local bookshops and www.poppyland.co.uk

CPSIA information can be obtained
at www.ICGtesting.com
Printed in the USA
LVHW011613050721
691876LV00011B/1365

9 781909 796782